The Penguin First Certificate Course

Student's Book

The Penguin First Certificate Course

Student's Book

Michael Thorn

Penguin Books

Penguin Books Ltd, Harmondsworth, Middlesex, England
Viking Penguin Inc., 40 West 23rd Street, New York, New York 10010, U.S.A.
Penguin Books Australia Ltd, Ringwood, Victoria, Australia
Penguin Books Canada Limited, 2801 John Street, Markham, Ontario, Canada L3R 1B4
Penguin Books (N.Z.) Ltd, 182–190 Wairau Road, Auckland 10, New Zealand

First published 1987

Typeset, printed and bound in Great Britain by
Hazell Watson & Viney Limited,
Member of the BPCC Group,
Aylesbury, Bucks

Typeset in Century Schoolbook

Designed by Gillian Riley

Contents

Acknowledgements

For permission to reproduce copyright material, the publishers gratefully acknowledge the following:

Michael Joseph Ltd for the extract from *Odds Against* by Dick Francis, page 16; the Hutchinson Publishing Group Ltd for the extract from 'The Venus Fly Trap' from *The Fallen Curtain and Other Stories* by Ruth Rendell, page 65; A. D. Peters & Co. Ltd for the extract from *Gifts of Passage* by Santha Rama Rau, page 94; Genesis Public Relations Ltd for the Miss Dylon shoe colour instructions, page 122; Harrison of Birmingham Ltd for the article on the art of window dressing, page 154.

Introduction

This course is designed to prepare students for the Cambridge First Certificate examination. It consists of twelve units and four tests.

Each unit is divided into sections which, together, cover the five papers in the examination. Some of these sections practise skills directly related to the examination, such as reading and listening comprehension, essay writing and interview technique. Others are concerned with grammar revision, vocabulary extension and communicative activities, all of which are equally important when preparing for the examination.

While following the course, you are advised to read as widely as possible (books or English newspapers) in order to increase your vocabulary and to become familiar with a variety of texts. In addition, you should take every opportunity of listening to native English speakers, perhaps by tuning in to the BBC World Service and watching English and American television programmes or films. This will not only provide you with extra comprehension practice, but will help to improve your own pronunciation and intonation as well.

As with all examinations, it is impossible to predict exactly what each paper will contain. However, with careful study and sufficient practice, you should be able to approach the examination with confidence, and it only remains for me to wish you all the very best of luck.

Finally, I am most grateful to Susan Firman and Hermione Ieronymidis for all their hard work and helpful advice.

Michael Thorn
London, 1986

●● = This material is recorded

Unit 1   Home Computers

A Reading comprehension

Study the following words and phrases before you read the text.

installing fitting
invest in put money into
their equipment the computer and software
to establish to set up
a card-index system a filing system in which the information to be stored is written on cards
a device an instrument

Read the text quickly and find the answers to these questions:

1 What are people doing with micro-computers?

2 Why do children usually want one?

3 Why is it a good idea to connect the computer to a telephone?

Home Computers

A quiet revolution is taking place. More and more families are installing micro-computers in their homes and beginning to discover what they can do with them.

The reasons why a family may decide to invest in a home micro vary. Fre-
5 quently it is little Johnny, the twelve-year-old, who persuades his parents to pay the £3–400 necessary. Johnny wants the computer so that he can play computer games, of course. His parents know exactly why he wants it, but hope that by playing games he will become familiar with computers. This may happen, although there is a lot of difference between playing games and
10 writing original programs.

If one or other of Johnny's parents uses a computer in the office, there is a good chance that the family will begin to use their equipment for more interesting purposes than just playing games. But this rarely happens until people learn to 'think computer'.

15 Let us imagine that Johnny's father has a record collection which he wishes to index. If he is familiar with computers, it is only natural that he should use the computer to store the information. If not he will more probably use some sort of card-index system. In this instance there are considerable advantages in using the computer, which will give him the information he
20 requires more quickly and efficiently than would a card-index system.

If Johnny's parents are computer people, they will know, too, that a simple device fixed to the telephone will enable them to obtain a wide variety of information, from what's on at the theatre to the latest sports news or the price of a holiday in the sun. And this is only the beginning. Whether we like
25 the idea or not, the home computer is here to stay.

Now read the text carefully and answer the following:

4 Why are parents prepared to spend a lot of money on a computer when they know their children only want to use it for computer games?

5 What sort of family is likely to benefit most from having a computer in the home?

6 What advantages do you think there might be in indexing the record collection on a computer rather than using a card-index system?

7 What sort of information can be obtained by linking a computer to a telephone?

8 Can you think of any further information you could obtain by linking a computer to a telephone?

B Multiple choice questions

Choose the best answer.

1 Parents may decide to buy a micro-computer

a hoping that the children will benefit.
b hoping that the children will use it for computer games.
c hoping to find out what to do with it.
d hoping to learn how to play computer games.

2 Johnny's father

a would use a card-index system if he knew about computers.
b would use a card-index system if he didn't know about computers.
c might use a card-index system if he knew about computers.
d might use a card-index system if he didn't know about computers.

3 a You can get information from a computer but not without a telephone.
b By connecting a computer to a telephone you can get information.
c You can't get information from a computer unless you connect it to a telephone.
d Without a computer you can't get any information.

C Word study

Either the noun or the verb form of the following words was used in the text.
Complete the two lists.

Noun	Verb
1	install
2	discover
3	decide
4	invest
5	persuade
6	know
7	hope
8 equipment	....
9	imagine
10 collection	....

Now answer the following questions:

11 They are installing a new X in the hospital. What might X be?

12 The d......................... changed the lives of all the people who lived there. What do you think they discovered?

13 People often decide to change their job. Think of some reasons for this d......................... .

14 The company is investing a great deal of money in a new Y. What might Y be?

15 They frequently try to persuade us to buy things we don't need. Suggest who *they* might be.

16 He doesn't know much Spanish, so his k......................... of Spanish is limited.

17 Where are you hoping to go for your next holiday?

18 Unfortunately they had a lot of equipment and it was very heavy. Who do you think *they* were and what was the equipment for?

19 If he was late home she always imagined that something awful had happened. She had a lot of i................. . What sort of things did she imagine had happened?

20 He has a large collection of butterflies. What do you think he does in the summer?

D Word study

Look at the following from the text:

Frequently it is little Johnny who persuades his parents to buy a computer. (ll. 4–5) But this **rarely** happens until . . . (l. 13)

Both **frequently** and **rarely** belong to a useful group of adverbs which we use when we want to say how often things happen. Here are some more:

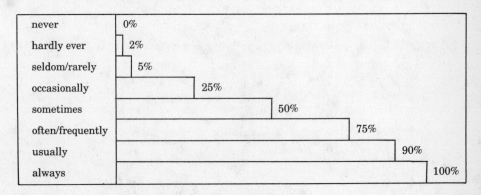

never	0%
hardly ever	2%
seldom/rarely	5%
occasionally	25%
sometimes	50%
often/frequently	75%
usually	90%
always	100%

Study these short descriptions of three characters:

1 Bernard, a successful fifty-year-old businessman, rather overweight, who drives a big car.

2 Linda, a twenty-five-year-old housewife with a three-month-old baby.

3 Tony, an unemployed young man of seventeen who is a keen amateur boxer.

Work in pairs and decide how often each of these characters might:

go jogging	travel by car
get up early in the morning	travel by bus
travel abroad	go to the theatre
eat in expensive restaurants	watch television
smoke	go to bed very late

Note that all the adverbs listed above come *before* the verb when used in statements.

Example I should imagine Tony **often** goes jogging.

E Focus on grammar: present simple; present continuous

Look at the picture. Then answer the questions.

1   What are the girls doing? (Think of several answers.) They are . . .

2   How do you know that the girl standing up is feeling happy?
    Because she . . .

3   Where do you think the girls come from?
    I think they . . .

4   What language do you imagine they speak?
    I imagine they . . .

5   Do any of the girls wear glasses?
    Yes, the girl . . .

6   How do you know?
    Because she . . .

The answer to question **2** is: Because she is smiling.
This is what the girl was doing **at the moment when the photograph was taken**.

The answer to question **5** is: The girl on the left wears glasses.
Here we are speaking about something **that is generally true about this girl**.

What about questions **1, 3, 4** and **6**?

Here are some more examples from the reading text.

a A quiet revolution **is taking place**. (l. 1)

More and more families **are installing** micro-computers in their homes and [**they are**] **beginning to discover** . . . (ll. 1–2)

To express the idea of something happening at or around the present moment we use the present continuous.

Examples Look. **The tide is coming in**.

Oh, dear, **it's raining**. We're going to get wet.

b Frequently it is little Johnny, the twelve-year-old, **who persuades** his parents to pay the £3—400 . . . (ll. 4–6)

His parents know exactly why **he wants** it, but [**they**] **hope** that . . . (ll. 6–7)

The present simple is often used with adverbs such as: seldom, often, frequently, sometimes, never, usually, always.

Examples **Sylvia never eats** meat.

Do you often go to the seaside?

Notice that both these examples refer to a habitual action.

The present simple is also used to express general truths.

Example **Africans don't all speak** the same language.

F *Grammar practice*

1 *Work in pairs. Think of one thing that each of these people does:*

a An airline pilot . . .
b A bank clerk . . .
c A dancer . . .
d A politician . . .
e A butcher . . .
f A landlady . . .
g A fisherman . . .
h A hairdresser . . .
i A dentist . . .
j A plumber . . .

Compare your answers with those of the students sitting next to you.

2 If you stay at a big hotel you expect the service to be good, but often you don't really notice the people who do all the things that ensure that the service *is* good. *Think of some of the things that the staff of a big hotel do every day.*

Examples They welcome the guests.

They show them to their rooms.

G Writing activity

In order to do well in the First Certificate examination, you will have to learn to express your ideas clearly and accurately in written English.

Remember　We begin the first word of a sentence with a capital letter and we end the sentence with a full stop. The comma is used to break up longer and more complex sentences.

Example　Small shops are usually friendly places. These days, however, many people prefer to buy their groceries at a supermarket, where they have a very wide choice. At a supermarket you can buy tea, biscuits, rice and many other items.

This is the sort of short essay question you will find in the examination:
Write 120–180 words on 'Is there a future for the corner shop?'

Here is a suggested answer to that question. You will notice that the writer has used three paragraphs. In the first he talks about shopping at the supermarket. In the second he explains why the corner shop may continue to be useful. In the third he says what he thinks will happen in the future.

Rewrite the essay, putting in the necessary capital letters, full stops and commas.

in a good supermarket we can buy nearly all the things we need prices are reasonable and we don't have to wait a long time to be served we can park behind the store and load up our trolley or basket with the things we want and usually we have a wide choice

sometimes however we may forget something in the supermarket or perhaps we suddenly run out of sugar or coffee then it is very useful to have a corner shop near our home if we go there regularly the shopkeeper is pleased to see us and the atmosphere is very friendly.

in the future i think that supermarkets will become bigger and bigger and often be situated outside the centre of the big cities i believe that the corner shop will survive however it has an important part to play in the life of the community

H *Listening comprehension*

Listen carefully to the conversation, then fill in the missing information on the envelope:

	Palace Theatre
This envelope contains . . . tickets.	Price of seats:
Production: *The Dancing Years*	Seat numbers:
Day and date of performance:	Address:
Name of purchaser:	
Please note The performance starts at	

I *Communicative practice: permission*

May we . . .?	Yes, of course.
Are we allowed to . . .?	Yes, certainly.
Do you think we could . . .?	No, I'm afraid not.
Could we possibly . . .?	No, I'm afraid that's not possible.

A *Model conversations*

1 a May we light a fire? **or** Are we allowed to light a fire?

b Yes, of course. **or** No, I'm afraid not.

Work in pairs. Use the phrases in the box to make similar conversations.

> use the tennis court
> borrow the tennis balls
> make some coffee
> watch television
> ride the ponies

2 a Could we possibly borrow the typewriter? **or** Do you think we could borrow the typewriter?

b Yes, certainly. **or** No, I'm afraid that's not possible.

Continue working in pairs. Use the phrases in the box to make similar conversations.

> use the record player
> watch the horror movie
> pick some of the plums
> have some tea
> see the photographs

B

1 a *Look at the picture above. Imagine you and your class are on a camping holiday. Practise using different ways of asking permission. The prompts below will help you.*

1 go . . . –ing

2 borrow . . .

3 go . . . –ing

4 pick . . .

5 light . . .

6 go . . .

7 play . . .

8 picnic . . .

b *Imagine you are staying with an English-speaking family as a guest. Think of some occasions when you might wish to ask permission to do things. What would you say?*

J Writing activity

On 10 May it is your birthday. You want to give a party, but you live in a small flat and the neighbours always complain if you make any noise.

Your friend James lives in a big house with his parents. There is a room at the back where he held his last birthday party. James's hi-fi system is much better than yours.

Write to James and ask if you can hold your birthday party at his house.

You will need 80–120 words.

Unit 2   Odds Against

A Reading comprehension

Study the following words and phrases before you read the text.

Telephoning for the local taxi . . .' is another way of saying 'I telephoned for the local taxi . . .'
tackled the problem dealt with the problem
we sorted out we found, we decided on
crumpets you eat toasted crumpets hot, with butter, at teatime
. . . who began sharpening her claws she began to attack him by making nasty remarks

Read the text quickly and find the answers to these questions:

1   What was the physical handicap suffered by the man telling the story?

2   Who put the film into the camera?

3   Do you think Mrs van Dysart and the man telling the story liked one another?

Odds Against

Telephoning for the local taxi to come and fetch me, I went to Oxford and bought a camera. Although it was the start of a busy Saturday afternoon, the boy who served me tackled the problem of a one-handed photographer with enthusiasm and as if he had all the time in the world. Between us we
5   sorted out a miniature German sixteen millimetre camera, three inches long by one and a half wide, which I could hold, set, snap, and wind with one hand with the greatest of ease.

He gave me a thorough lesson in how to work it, added an inch to its length in the shape of a screwed-on photo-electric light meter, loaded it with film,
10   and slid it into a black case so small that it made no bulge in my trouser pocket. He also offered to change the film later if I couldn't manage it. We parted on the best of terms.

When I got back everyone was sitting round a cosy fire in the drawing-room eating crumpets. Very tantalizing. I loved crumpets.

15   No one took much notice when I went in and sat down on the fringe of the circle except Mrs van Dysart, who began sharpening her claws. She got in a couple of quick digs about young men marrying girls for their money, and Charles didn't say that I hadn't. Viola looked at me searchingly, worry opening her mouth. I winked, and she shut it again in relief.

From *Odds Against* by Dick Francis.

Now read the text carefully and answer the following:

4 Why was the camera recommended by the assistant particularly suitable?

5 How did the light meter fix onto the camera?

6 What did the assistant suggest he might do for the writer that he wouldn't normally do for a customer?

7 How many crumpets did the writer eat? How do you know?

8 It is suggested that Charles disappointed the writer. How?

9 How do you know that the writer and Viola were fond of one another?

B Multiple choice questions

Choose the best answer.

1 The writer
a lived in Oxford.
b was staying in Oxford.
c was staying near Oxford.
d was brought home from Oxford in a taxi.

2 The assistant in the shop
a had plenty of time.
b was particularly helpful.
c was used to selling cameras to one-armed photographers.
d considered one-armed photographers a problem.

3 The assistant
a showed the writer how to fix the light meter.
b taught the writer how to use the camera.
c put the camera into the writer's pocket.
d demonstrated how to load the film.

4 When the writer got back to the house
a he ate some crumpets.
b he sat down on the floor with the others.
c Mrs van Dysart said something unpleasant.
d Charles joined in the discussion.

5 Viola
a was looking for something.
b was searching for the writer.
c didn't know who the writer was.
d knew the writer well.

C Word study

Choose the word or phrase which best completes the sentence:

1 The shop where he bought the camera was full .... people because it
   was Saturday.
   a of **b** off **c** up **d** with

2 My aunt is arriving this evening. Could you possibly .... her from the
   station?
   a handle **b** fetch **c** hand **d** carry

3 The customs officer searched the cases ....
   a thoroughly **b** thorough **c** complete **d** hardly

4 The tiger had very sharp ....
   a feet **b** paws **c** nails **d** claws

5 I don't really like the way meals are .... in this restaurant.
   a serviced **b** dished **c** dined **d** served

6 Maurice .... down the hill on the sledge.
   a slip **b** slide **c** slid **d** slipped

7 Don't move. I warn you, this revolver is ....
   a loaded **b** pointed **c** aimed **d** shelled

8 We must .... who is going to be responsible for selling the tickets.
   a sort through **b** sort out **c** make out **d** think out

D Word study

We use adjectives to describe nouns.

Examples He gave me a **thorough** lesson . . . (l. 8)
. . . and slid it into a **black** case . . . (l. 10)

Study these sentences containing more useful adjectives:

The exam was an **absolute** disaster for Frank.
I want you to give me an **accurate** account of everything that happens.
Although she is eighty-two years old, she still leads a very **active** life.
That is the **actual** house where Shakespeare was born.
There is an **additional** charge of 15 per cent for service.
I think the pay is **adequate**.
He made some very **aggressive** remarks.
She gets very **anxious** if the children are home late.
A bowl filled with **artificial** flowers stood on a table by the window.
What an **astonishing** bit of news!
They have a very **attractive** home.
There was an **awful** storm last night.

Now complete the following dialogue using some of the adjectives on page 18:

'You've dined at the (1) .... restaurant where the incident took place, haven't you? How did you find the service?'

'I suppose it was (2) ...., although the waiters were very slow and they became quite (3) .... if you tried to hurry them up. Personally I thought the food was (4) ...., and when I asked for the bill I found there was an (5) .... charge of 10 per cent for service. The restaurant itself is very (6) .... of course, with that view across the lake, but I must say I find it (7) .... that it was given three stars in the food guide. I should have thought one star would have been a more (8) .... rating.'

'I agree entirely.'

E Word study

We use adverbs to modify verbs, adjectives and other adverbs.

Examples   Viola looked at me **searchingly**. (l. 18)
It was a **very** small camera.
The taxi moved **terribly** slowly up the street.

Replace the words and phrases in **bold** *type with adverbs formed from the list of adjectives in section D.*

Example   The man was **very** thin.
The man was **awfully** thin.

1 His story was **completely** true.
2 He approached the detective **in a worried manner**.
3 The books were **surprisingly** cheap.
4 She is, **by her personal actions**, supporting the party.
5 Mrs Peters is an **extremely** rich woman.
6 The steak was cooked **reasonably well**.
7 'If I were you, I wouldn't ask so many questions,' said the man with the moustache **in a threatening manner**.
8 The lady was **in fact** the gentleman's wife.
9 He added up the bill **without making any mistakes**.
10 They've furnished their home very **nicely**.

F Focus on grammar: past simple; past continuous

Look at this sentence from the text:

When I **got** back everyone **was sitting** round a cosy fire in the drawing-room . . . (l. 13)

This is a typical example of the past simple and past continuous tenses being used together.
We use the past continuous tense for an action which continued for a period of time in the past. Very often this action is **interrupted** by another action in the simple past.

Compare **a** I **came** downstairs when the taxi driver *rang* the bell.
b I **was coming** downstairs when the taxi driver *rang* the bell.
In sentence **a** the taxi driver rang the bell and the speaker then came downstairs.
In sentence **b** the action of coming downstairs was interrupted by the sound of the doorbell.

G Grammar practice

Practise expressing more ideas as in section F. Use one verb in the past simple and one in the past continuous tense. Remember, the past simple will not always come first.

1 When I/house/Charles and Viola/their dinner.
2 I/my new camera/when Charles/into my room.
3 When I/downstairs/Mrs van Dysart/to her husband.
4 I/the film/when Viola/at my door.
5 The next morning/I/the newspaper in the garden/when/postman.
6 I/my letter/when Charles/downstairs.
7 I/my breakfast/when Viola/the news.
8 I/into the hall to ring for a taxi/but Mrs van Dysart/the phone.
9 When she/the phone down/Mrs van Dysart/worried.
10 Viola/to Charles/when I/the sitting-room.

H Grammar practice

Sometimes we use a series of verbs in the past continuous tense to describe the scene of some action that is to follow.

Look at this example:

It was nearly 5 o'clock. Assistants were shutting and locking the street doors, the assistant manager was turning out the lights and the last customers were reluctantly leaving the store. Then suddenly the fire alarm sounded . . .

Put the verbs in brackets in the following text into the past simple or the past continuous.

As soon as Julia (1 enter) the hall she (2 realize) that she had arrived far too early. An elderly man (3 arrange) chairs on the platform and two sound engineers (4 check) the microphones. Meanwhile another man at the back of the hall (5 stand) at the very top of a tall ladder. He (6 do) something to the lights. The only members of the audience already in their seats were a young couple about Julia's age. They (7 turn) round and (8 glance) at her, then quickly (9 look) away.

Julia (10 choose) a seat at the end of a row half-way down the hall and (11 sit) down. She (12 think) of Tom. She wondered what he (13 do) at that moment; polishing up his speech no doubt. Would he be surprised to learn that she had accepted his invitation to attend the meeting?

I Discussion

Can you think of some items of electrical equipment you might expect to find in someone's home? Make a list.

If you had a home of your own and you could start off with THREE electrical items only, which would you choose? Explain why.

J Listening comprehension

The Electricity Board wants to find out what pieces of electrical equipment people use in their homes. *Listen to the interview and write in the details on the form.* The interviewer has already filled in one or two items for you. Don't worry if you don't catch everything the first time. You will hear the interview twice.

Name *Mr*			Address		Is this a flat or a house?	
Electrical items in home						
Kitchen	Sitting-room	Bedroom 1	Bedroom 2	Bedroom 3	Bathroom	Other rooms
Washing machine						

K Writing activity

Make all the changes and additions necessary to produce, from the following eight sets of words and phrases, eight sentences which will complete the letter.

Here is an example of the kind of alteration you will need to make:

I/be/very happy/if you/look into/matter immediately.

I would be very happy if you could look into this matter immediately.

```
                              10, George Street,
                              Bedford,
                              Beds.
                              14 June 19 -
      Dear Sir,
1     On 4 May/I/purchase/Globus washing machine/
      local branch/Tompkin's.

2     I/enclose/copy/receipt/and you/see/pay/cash.

3     My husband/remove/old washing machine/and two
      engineers/employ/Tompkin's/instal/new machine.

4     engineers/test/machine/which/appear/work well.

5     However/first time/I/turn on/machine/cause/
      flood/my kitchen.

6     I/telephone/Tompkin's/and/engineer who/come/look
      at/machine/blame/a faulty hose.

7     He/promise/order/replacement immediately.

8     That/be/six weeks ago/andI/be/still unable/use/
      my washing machine.

      Every time I telephone Tompkin's they tell me
      that you have still not sent them the new hose.
      Really I do not know what to believe, but I would
      be grateful if you could contact them immediately
      and sort this matter out.

      Yours faithfully,

      Janet Nelson
```

L Interview

1 *Look at the photograph, then answer the questions:*

a Where do you think the people are?
b What are they doing?
c What time of year do you think it is? Give reasons for your answer.
d Do you think any of the people in the picture are related to one another? Why/why not?
e If you had the choice would you prefer to spend a day at the seaside or a day in the country? Give your reasons.
f What sort of things do you like doing when you are on holiday?
g Can you remember a particular holiday that you enjoyed very much? Where did you go? What did you do?

2 *Study the three holiday advertisements below. Then say in your own words what each holiday has to offer. Talk about the geographic location, the scenery and the things people would be able to do there.*

a Normandy – France.
Normandy offers a wealth of interest in its countryside, beaches and historic towns. The holiday will be based in Bayeux, a typical French town, unspoilt by tourism. The excursion programme will provide some easy walking in the countryside and on the shores and cliffs of Normandy.

b Sorrento and Rome – Italy.
This spectacular holiday combines the scenic beauty of the Bay of Naples with the glories of ancient Rome. Our hotel overlooks the bay and our excursion programme includes visits to Capri, the crater of Vesuvius and the ruins of Pompeii.

c Ulvik – Norway.
Ulvik enjoys a sheltered position overlooking a fjord. The scenery is varied – farmland, forests and mountains. It is situated in the centre of the fruit growing area of Norway. We arrange a full programme of excursions by boat and bus, or you can just relax on the sun terrace and enjoy the view.

If you had a choice, which of these holidays would you choose? Give your reasons.

M Writing activity

The following is a typical essay question:

Write 120–160 words on 'A holiday I remember well'.

Write three paragraphs. In the first, say where you went and how you got there. In the second, say what you did during your holiday. Your final paragraph should be short, perhaps a general comment on the holiday to conclude the essay.

Below is a specimen answer to the above question. It contains a number of ideas and the English is correct, but unfortunately the sentences have got into the wrong order.

Rewrite the essay using three paragraphs, according to the instructions above.

Switzerland is a beautiful country and one day I would like to go back and visit the Italian part. I remember one splendid trip we made to Schaffhausen, where we visited the famous Rhine Waterfall. We travelled by train to Zurich and were able to find a cheap hotel in the old part of the city. It was September, but the weather was still warm and sunny. Some years ago a friend and I spent a very pleasant holiday in Switzerland. Another day we went to St Gallen. That day it poured with rain, but we didn't mind. We bought special rail tickets so that we could travel by train to different places every day. We took a lot of photographs.

Unit 3　　The Blue Room

A Reading comprehension

Study the following words and phrases before you read the text.

being saddled with me being forced to have me with you
visiting the odd record shop visiting one or two record shops
shattered destroyed
a generation gap a big difference in our ages
the promenade the wide road facing the sea
slot machines machines with slots, or holes, into which coins are pushed
the pier the long platform built out over the sea
a compulsion a strong feeling that you *must* do something

Read the text quickly and find the answers to these questions:

1 Who suggested that Douglas and the writer should spend the morning together?

2 Why weren't there many people about?

3 What did Douglas want the money for?

The Blue Room

'All right,' said Douglas, 'I know you don't like being saddled with me, but it's only for this morning. I wish you'd try not to look quite so miserable about it.'

Douglas was my cousin and he was right, of course. I had planned to spend
5　the morning exploring the back streets of the seaside town, discovering one or two secondhand bookshops, visiting the odd record shop perhaps and then, at breakfast, my dream had been shattered by my Aunt.
'You're not busy this morning, are you Tom?' she said cheerfully, 'Why don't you take Douglas for a walk along the beach? I have some shopping to do.'
10　Since I, like my cousin, was staying at my Aunt's seaside home, it was a request that was impossible to refuse.

Douglas was eleven and I was more than twice that age. There was a serious generation gap. So here we were, strolling along the promenade on a grey, rather windy autumn morning, with little in common apart from vague
15　family ties.
'You don't really want to go for a walk along the beach, do you?' I asked.
'Not particularly,' said Douglas. 'Have you got any money?'
'How much?' I enquired suspiciously.
'A couple of pounds,' he replied.
20　'Probably,' I said.
'Then let's go to the Blue Room.'
'The Blue Room?' I'd never heard of it.
'At the end of the pier. Come on, I'll show you.'

Apart from one or two elderly couples wandering along arm in arm, the pier
25　was deserted. Empty deckchairs flapped forlornly in the breeze, and the doors of the seaside photographers, the fortune tellers and the souvenir shops were firmly shut and barred. But at the far end a large sign in flashing

coloured lights still invited the public to sample the 'Amusements'.
'Thank goodness it's still open,' said Douglas, increasing his pace.

30 My heart sank and I remembered the strange compulsion of my own youth
to feed pennies into slot machines and send little silver balls whizzing round
and round. By the time I was sixteen I had grown out of these games.
We went in through the double doors, under the illuminated sign.
'Give us a pound then,' Douglas was saying eagerly.

35 Mechanically I handed him a pound coin and he dashed off to change it into
10p pieces. I looked about me and realized at once that this was a world I
knew nothing of. Oh, there were one or two fruit machines which seemed
familiar, but what was this strange game called 'Frogger'? 'Help the frog
across the road', while the electronic vehicles thundered by, or 'The mad
40 planet', where multicoloured spacecraft sped through a starry universe,
constantly under attack from small, evil-looking machines, where the air
was filled with the roar of gigantic explosions and the spacecraft suddenly
disintegrated in huge sheets of flame.

Douglas was back at my side, his eyes shining. 'Good, isn't it?' he said. 'Got
45 another pound?'

Now read the text carefully and answer the following:

4 What was the writer's reaction when it was suggested that he and Douglas should spend the morning together?

5 What had the writer been looking forward to doing?

6 How does Douglas indicate that he realizes the writer would prefer to be alone?

7 What is the relationship between Douglas and the writer?

8 Why do you think the deckchairs were unoccupied?

9 What caused the writer to stop playing slot machines?

10 Why did Douglas change the pound coin the writer gave him into 10p pieces?

11 Why does the writer say 'this was a world I knew nothing of'?

12 Explain why Douglas's eyes were shining.

B Multiple choice questions

Choose the best answer.

1 a Douglas didn't want to spend the morning with the writer.
  b Douglas wanted to explore the back streets of the town.
  c The writer wanted to go shopping with his aunt.
  d The writer wasn't happy at the thought of spending the morning with his cousin.

2 a The writer suggested they should walk along the beach.
  b The writer's aunt suggested they should go for a walk along the promenade.
  c Douglas wanted to know how much money the writer had.
  d Douglas suggested they should go to the Blue Room.

3 a There was nobody on the pier.
  b There was a fortune teller on the pier.
  c Most of the souvenir shops were shut.
  d Douglas was relieved to discover that the pier was not closed.

4 When the writer stepped inside the Blue Room

  a he was amazed.
  b he was excited.
  c he was shocked.
  d he was upset.

5 Inside the Blue Room

  a it was crowded.
  b it was dangerous.
  c it was noisy.
  d it was hot.

C *Word study*

*Use a form of the words in **bold** type in the margin to fill the blank spaces.*

Examples   **plan**   I had   *planned*   to spend the morning writing letters.

        discover   The   *discovery*   was made when builders were repairing a wall.

request   **1**   My .... to speak to the minister was turned down.

shatter   **2**   All the windows at the front of the building were .... by the force of the explosion.

stroll   **3**   'Come on,' said John, 'let's go for a .... in the park.'

explore   **4**   Further .... of the site revealed the tiled floor of a Roman bathhouse.

refuse   **5**   He was sent to prison for ten years, largely as a result of his .... to name the other members of the gang.

enquire   **6**   Thank you for your .... Unfortunately we are unable to help.

bar   **7**   An enormous man stood in the doorway .... our way. 'Yes, gentlemen,' he said, 'can I help you?'

speed   **8**   We stood miserably at the side of the motorway, as the homebound traffic .... by.

explode   **9**   The bomb landed right in front of the house, but fortunately it never ....

flash   **10**   Of course this photograph here was taken using ....

D Word study

Note the following from the text:

So here we were, **strolling** along the promenade . . . (l. 13)
. . . he **dashed** off to change it . . . (l. 35)
. . . elderly couples **wandering** along . . . (l. 24)
. . . and send little silver balls **whizzing** round . . . (l. 31)

Here are some more verbs that describe some of the ways things and people move:

creep, crawl, cross, disintegrate, flap, flash, jump, hop, hurry, limp, march, skid, speed, stride, sway, thunder.

Work in pairs. Check the meaning of any of these words you don't understand in your dictionary. Make sure you know the simple past form. Use fourteen of the verbs above in the correct form to complete the following sentences:

1 Sorry, we must .... or we'll miss our train.

2 The lights turned to green and the pedestrians .... the road.

3 Tom and Alice stood at the side of the motorway, while the great lorries .... by.

4 The children's game involved standing on one leg and .... from one square to another.

5 The washing hanging on the line .... in the wind.

6 The injured tennis player .... off the court.

7 The force of the explosion caused the yellow van completely to ....

8 The boys .... on to their bikes and cycled away.

9 The headmaster .... on to the platform. He looked furious.

10 The railway track was uneven and the train .... from side to side as it entered the tunnel.

11 The baby .... out through the bedroom door to the top of the stairs.

12 The soldiers .... out of the barracks.

13 Trying to make as little noise as possible, John .... up the stairs.

14 Away to the west the lightning ...., and Peter heard the sound of thunder.

E Focus on grammar: **past perfect**

Look at the following sentences from the reading text:

. . . he was right, of course. I **had planned** to spend the morning . . . (ll. 4–5)

By the time I was sixteen I **had grown out of** these games. (l. 32)

We use the past perfect tense (had + past participle) when we want to express the idea that one event in the past happened before another.

Look at some more examples:

First he washed and shaved. Then he went downstairs.

As soon as he **had washed and shaved**, he went downstairs.

He **had worked** as a mechanic for four years before they let him drive one of the racing cars.

After the detectives **had checked** the window for fingerprints, they searched the garden.

F Grammar practice

Put the verbs in the following sentences into the past simple or the past perfect tense:

1 It was only after Jackie (see) the film that she (decide) to read the book.

2 He (not realize) his mistake until after he (post) the letter.

3 I (just make) a pot of tea when Miriam (arrive).

4 She (not notice) that the money (go) until some hours later.

5 I (wait) impatiently for Felix. I (not see) him for more than ten years.

6 From her handbag she (take) the letter he (write) to her twenty years earlier.

7 Clark (meet) Rogers again in Durban. By this time Rogers (join) a small circus.

8 Logan (not say) anything until I (finish) my story.

9 The moment Simpson (enter) the room, he noticed that the clock (stop) at eight o'clock precisely.

10 Why you (not tell) your father you (sell) the stamps?

G *Focus on grammar:* **reported speech 1**

There are two ways of reporting what somebody says.

We can use direct speech: e.g. Douglas said, 'I don't want to go on the beach.'

Or we can use reported speech: e.g. Douglas said he didn't want to go on the beach.

When we change direct speech into reported speech, **present tense** becomes **past tense** and **past tense** and **present perfect tenses** become **past perfect tense**. Certain other things change, too. Study this chart.

Direct speech	Reported speech
Douglas: 'I **like** this cake.'	Douglas *said* he **liked** that cake.
Mary: 'Do you often **travel** by train?'	Mary *asked* if I often **travelled** by train.
John: 'I **posted** that letter myself.'	John *told* me he **had posted** the letter himself.
Emily: 'I **met** Maureen yesterday.'	Emily *remarked* that she **had met** Maureen the day before.
Ted: 'I **have broken** my watch.'	Ted *announced* that he **had broken** his watch.
Arthur: '**Have** you ever **been** to France?'	Arthur *wanted to know* if I **had** ever **been** to France.

Notice that all the reporting verbs are in the past. When the reporting verb is in the present there is no change of tense.

Example   Douglas: 'I **like** this chocolate.'
Douglas *says* he **likes** this chocolate.

H *Grammar practice*

When Tom and Douglas got home, Tom's aunt asked him about their walk.
Report their conversation.
The first question has been done for you.

Aunt   Did you enjoy your walk?
Tom's aunt asked if they had enjoyed their walk.

Tom   Er . . . yes, we did.
1   Tom replied that . . .

Aunt   Where did you go?
2   Tom's aunt wanted to know . . .

Tom		We walked as far as the pier.
	3	Tom told her . . .
Aunt		Oh, did you see the lifeboat?
	4	Tom's aunt asked . . .
Tom		Er . . . we visited a place called the Blue Room.
	5	Tom told her . . .
Aunt		The Blue Room? I've never heard of it. What did you do there?
	6	Tom's aunt said . . . She asked . . .
Tom		We played electronic games. I haven't been in one of those places for years.
	7	Tom informed her . . . He said . . .
Aunt		Do you have to pay to use the machines?
	8	Tom's aunt enquired . . .
Tom		Oh, they are quite expensive.
	9	Tom told her . . .
Aunt		I hope Douglas wasn't bored.
	10	Tom's aunt said she . . ., but Tom assured her that Douglas had enjoyed himself very much.

I Listening comprehension

You are going to hear a news broadcast. Listen carefully, then answer the questions. You will hear the broadcast twice.

Write the missing word in each of these headlines:

1 Two people were .... in a fire at a hotel near Victoria Station.

2 Unemployment figures are down for the third .... month.

3 House prices are expected to .... by 5 per cent this year.

4 The boom in the .... of home computers continues.

5 Italian drivers will .... the first four places on the grid for the Brazilian Grand Prix.

Tick (√) whether the following are true or false:

		True	False
6	Some people were killed in a fire.		
7	The alarm was given by a bus conductor.		
8	Fewer people will draw unemployment benefit this month than last.		
9	House prices will probably increase by more than 5 per cent in some places this year.		
10	There is a greater demand for houses in the south than in the south west.		
11	Last year approximately 66,000 home computers were sold in Britain.		
12	There are three cars on each row of the grid for the Brazilian Grand Prix.		

J Writing activity

Listen again to the news story about the fire at a hotel near Victoria Station. Make notes if you wish. Then write your own account of what happened. You will need between 50 and 75 words.

K Communicative practice: suggestions

Shall we . . .?	All right, if you like.
Let's . . .	That's a good idea.
Why don't we . . .?	I'm afraid I can't.
How about —ing?	I don't think that's a very good
I thought we might . . .	idea.

Model conversations

1 a Let's listen to that new tape you bought.

b That's a good idea.   *or*   I don't think that's a very good idea. It's terribly late.

Work in pairs. Use the phrases in the box to make similar conversations. If you decide not to agree with the suggestion, give a reason.

have some coffee
put on a record
make some toast
go and see Charlie
listen to the news
try out the new computer

2 a Oh, dear. I've got problems with my car again.

b Why don't you buy a new one?

a I don't know. I might have to.

Continue working in pairs. Use the phrases in the box to make similar conversations. **a** *will have to think of alternative solutions.*

problems with my girl-friend/boy-friend
problems with my bank manager
problems with my knee
problems with my boss

3 a I thought we might go to the theatre tomorrow.

b I'm afraid I can't, not tomorrow.

a What about Saturday?

b All right, if you like.

Continue working in pairs. Use the phrases in the box to make similar conversations.

to the seaside/Saturday
to see Roger/this evening
to the museum/this afternoon
to the swimming pool/Wednesday

Here are two more situations. Think of as many suggestions as you can for each.
Then, in groups of three, make suggestions or respond to those of others.

a Three friends arrive at the central railway station of a big city, only to discover that the last train has left. They live about six miles from the centre.

b A friend is in urgent need of £2,000 and asks for your advice. He/she rents a flat, runs a car and has a life insurance policy that he/she took out nine years ago. His/her parents are still alive and his/her sister, who is married, lives in New York.

●● L Dialogue

Listen to the dialogue twice, without looking at it. Then answer the following questions:

1 What is Mrs Barclay's job?

2 What is she going to do?

3 How does George know it will soon be her birthday?

4 What are the four things that are suggested as possible birthday presents for Mrs Barclay?

5 Which suggestion do they finally agree on?

6 Why does Alice call George 'sexist'?

Narrator	George, Cindy, Tom and Alice work in a solicitor's office. Mrs Barclay is the lady responsible for keeping the office clean.
George	Quiet, please. I have an announcement.
Alice	A rise. We're all going to get a rise.
George	(*ignoring Alice*) Next Tuesday is Mrs Barclay's birthday.
Cindy	How do you know?
George	She reminded me; and you know what that means. Every year, on her birthday, Mrs Barclay brings in a birthday cake.
Alice	So we've got to buy her a present.
George	Exactly. Any ideas?
Cindy	Not easy. Mrs Barclay's the sort of person who has everything.
Tom	Why don't we get her a big bottle of perfume?
Alice	That's not a bad idea.
George	(*doubtfully*) Does Mrs Barclay use perfume?

Alice	I'm sure she does. Anyway it would make a nice present, wouldn't it?
George	What about one of those gift sets with soap and bathsalts and perfume all in one box.
Cindy	I'm afraid she might just leave it in the box . . . you know . . . not open it because it looked so nice . . .
Tom	Something to eat then. Let's get her something to eat.
Alice	All right, if you like. Chocolates. What about a nice, big box of chocolates?
Tom	Actually I was thinking of biscuits. I thought we might get her one of those big tins with all kinds of assorted biscuits.
Cindy	That seems a good idea. O.K.? Everyone agree? (*Vague sounds of agreement*)
George	Fine . . . shopping's a woman's job, so perhaps you and Alice could get something suitable?
Alice	Sexist . . . (*laughter*)

M Writing activity

Write a letter thanking someone for sending you a birthday present. You will need between 100 and 140 words, including your own address and the date.

Write three paragraphs. In the first, thank your friend for the present and write something pleasant about it. In the second, say how you spent your birthday. In the third, ask for news of your friend and suggest that you should meet some time.

Test 1

To be done without the aid of a dictionary.
No looking back to earlier sections of the book allowed.

Time 1 hour 30 minutes

Total possible marks 75

Ratings

55 marks or above:	**Good**
40 marks or above:	**Fair**
39 marks or less:	**Disappointing**. You are advised to spend some time revising Units 1–3.

A

Choose the word or phrase which best completes the sentence:

1 We hardly .... go out in the evening now.
a are **b** never **c** not **d** ever

2 I noticed that you .... working late last night.
a was **b** be **c** were **d** are

3 He .... back to the shop just before it closed.
a reached **b** got **c** arrived **d** appeared

4 Excuse me, I must sort .... these invitations.
a out **b** in **c** up **d** down

5 He .... her to try a new kind of soap powder.
a said **b** told **c** persuade **d** offered

6 The butcher gave me a lesson .... cutting the meat properly.
a in **b** to **c** of **d** from

7 When you go down the road, do you think you could .... my paper?
a carry **b** search **c** fetch **d** find

8 She looked at her husband ....
a friendly **b** worried **c** anxiously **d** astonished

9 We don't really have much .... common.
a on **b** in **c** to **d** as

10 The cowboy .... onto his horse and rode off.
a strode **b** jumped **c** hopped **d** limped

10 marks

B   *The words in the left-hand margin can be used to form a word that fits in the blank space in each sentence. Fill each space in this way:*

Example **know**   I'm afraid I have very little *knowledge* of this subject.

collect   1   He has a large .... of stamps.

equip   2   There is a lot of expensive .... in the laboratory.

enter   3   The main .... is round the other side of the building.

prefer   4   His .... for classical music soon became obvious.

refuse   5   She was angered by his .... to discuss the matter.

imagine   6   His work shows a lot of ....

invest   7   I wouldn't regard that as a good ....

discover   8   The .... of oil on the land affected the lives of all the people who lived there.

choose   9   Don't blame me. It was her own ....

decide   10   I feel we must make a .... today.

10 marks

C   *Report what these people said:*

Example   I'm not keen on these biscuits.
Tim said . . .
Tim said he wasn't keen on those biscuits.

1   I think your car is beautiful, Rosie.
Emma said . . .

6   I can't come on Saturday, Tom.
Gillian told . . .

2   I sent Mary a telegram.
John said . . .

7   This ice cream is delicious.
James says . . .

3   I've lost some money, Judy.
Larry told . . .

8   Do you ever travel by bus, Mr Scott?
Elsie asked . . .

4   Did you get my letter, Doris?
Prudence asked . . .

9   I gave June the letter myself.
Arthur tells me . . .

5   Have you visited Rome, Margaret?
Jim enquired . . .

10   The food is ready.
Jackie announced . . .

20 marks

D It's the first day of the course at a language school in the south of England. Max is talking to Yumiko. Fill in the blank spaces in the dialogue with a word or phrase:

Max Hello, my name's Max. I'm from Switzerland. Where (1) . . .?

Yumiko I come from Osaka, in Japan.

Max That's nice. Is (2) . . . day?

Yumiko Yes, it is. I only (3) . . . in England on Saturday.

Max Which airline (4) . . .?

Yumiko I came by Cathay Pacific.

Max Did (5) . . . Heathrow?

Yumiko Yes, we did. I must say, Heathrow is a very busy airport, isn't it?

Max I don't know. We landed at Gatwick. I came on a charter flight.

Yumiko Oh, I see. Was (6) . . .?

Max Well, it was a little cheaper than the scheduled flights, but still quite expensive. Are you (7) . . . English family?

Yumiko Yes, I am.

Max (8) . . . the food?

Yumiko Oh, it's very different from Japanese food.

Max I'm sure it is. (9) . . . a long way from the school?

Yumiko No, I can walk to school in five minutes.

Max You're lucky. I have to catch a bus in the morning. Oh, there's the bell. I tell you what, (10) . . . this interesting conversation after school. I'll wait for you by the front door. Bye.

Yumiko: Bye.

20 marks

E *You have been invited to a friend's birthday party. Unfortunately you are unable to go. Write, thanking your friend for the invitation and explaining why you won't be there. You will need 100–120 words.*

Don't forget to put *your* address and the date in the top right-hand corner.

15 marks

Unit 4 Texas Superstores

A Reading comprehension

Study the following words and phrases before you read the text.

open a credit account when you do this you can buy things and pay for them at a later date

interest if you borrow money you have to pay interest, so that eventually you pay back more than you borrowed

to clear your statement balance to pay all the money you owe

spread your repayments pay back a small amount of money each month

a higher credit limit permission to borrow more money

the outstanding balance the exact amount of money you owe

direct debit a system by which the bank will pay the store a fixed sum from your account each month

---

TEXAS SUPERSTORES

Seven good reasons why you ought to open a Texas Superstores credit account today:

1 You needn't carry large amounts of cash with you any more. The Texas Superstores credit card is the modern way of doing your shopping.

2 You will never have to pay a deposit for any purchase, however large, at one of our stores.

3 You may use your credit card in any Texas Superstores throughout Great Britain.

4 You won't pay anything until after you have used your card.

5 You pay no interest at all provided you clear your statement balance every month.

6 You may spread your repayments to suit yourself. This is obviously the most convenient way to pay.

7 You might wish to have a higher credit limit at some time. We shall grant your request with the minimum of fuss if we possibly can.

How do I open a Texas Superstores credit account?

Just complete the application form. Tick the spending limit you require, £250, £500 or more. The information which you give will be treated as strictly confidential.

Take the completed form to the Customer Accounts Office at any of our stores, where a member of our staff will go through it with you.

We'll send your application to our Head Office for formal approval, and your permanent, plastic card should reach you within a few days.

What will all this cost?

It costs you nothing to open an account and, provided that you pay for your purchases in full each month, you'll pay no interest at all. If, on the other hand, you decide to spread your repayments, we'll add a monthly charge of 2·5 per cent to your outstanding balance.

How do I make my repayments?

As soon as you've used your card to make a purchase, we'll start sending you monthly statements. You must pay a minimum of 5 per cent of the outstanding balance each month, although you may, of course, pay more if you wish.

You can pay at the Customer Accounts Office at any of our stores or send us a cheque through the post. On the other hand, if you have a bank account, you can pay us by direct debit. In this case your bank will automatically forward us the payment due each month.

So don't delay, apply today for your Texas Superstores credit card.

Read the text quickly and find the answers to these questions:

1 Why do you think Texas Superstores want people to open a credit account?

2 Why might somebody want a higher credit limit?

3 What would the customer do with the plastic card? What exactly is it for?

Now read the text carefully and answer the following:

4 Why will it no longer be necessary to carry a lot of cash?

5 Why do you think stores often ask for a deposit when they sell large items on credit?

6 In what circumstances could you make a purchase, yet pay no interest?

7 Why is spreading your payments a convenient way to pay?

8 In order to open a credit account you will be asked to give certain private information about yourself. How do you know that this information will not be given to other people?

9 What are the three ways of making repayments mentioned in the advertisement?

B *Multiple choice questions*

Choose the best answer.

1 Once you have a credit card

a you will no longer need to carry cash about with you.
b you will only have to pay the minimum deposit if you buy something at Texas Superstores.
c you will be in a position to purchase anything you want from Texas Superstores.
d you will be able to use your card at any Texas Superstores in England.

2 Texas Superstores

a will grant you a higher spending limit whenever you wish.
b will allow you credit not exceeding £500.
c won't charge you interest when you use your card.
d may be prepared to allow you credit in excess of £500.

3　When you open a Texas Superstores credit account

a　you must fill in the application form at the Customer Accounts office.
b　you must indicate how much credit you want.
c　you needn't decide at once on the spending limit you require.
d　you must send your completed form to the Customer Accounts office.

4　After you've used your card Texas Superstores

a　will send a statement to your bank showing how much you owe.
b　will send you a statement showing how much you've spent.
c　will send you a statement which you have to settle in full by the end of the following month.
d　will send a statement to your bank detailing the interest to be paid each month.

5　When making your repayments

a　you must send a cheque to Texas Superstores every month.
b　you must instruct your bank to pay by direct debit.
c　you must pay at least 5 per cent of the money you owe each month.
d　you must add 2·5 per cent to your repayments each month.

C Word study

Fill each of the numbered blanks in the following passage. Use only one word in each space.

Simon Grenfell was in bad trouble. He had (1) .... Mr Perkins, the Bank Manager, to (2) .... him £10,000 to finance a business venture (3) .... had gone disastrously wrong. He had already missed two (4) .... and now Mr Perkins had written, asking him to come and discuss the matter. With his letter Mr Perkins had enclosed a copy of Grenfell's (5) .... The young man glanced at it gloomily. He already (6) .... considerably more to the bank than the original sum he had (7) .... and he knew he had little (8) .... of being able to pay back any of the money at an early date. With (9) .... at around 20 per cent per year, his (10) .... would simply grow and grow until he was forced to (11) .... himself bankrupt. Should he consider taking this step immediately, he (12) .... ?

D Word study

Look at the following sentence from the text:

A member of our staff will **go through** it with you. (1.34–5)

We call verbs like **to go through** phrasal verbs. In the sentence above **to go through** means **to examine** or **to check**. It can also mean **to endure** or **to suffer**, as in this example: The shipwrecked sailors **went through** a terrible ordeal.

Phrasal verbs can be used in any tense. Here are some more examples, all of them using the particles **through** and **out of**.

The secretary **put through** a call to Mr Johnson.
Turner was lying, but the detectives soon **saw through** his story.
She's looking specially cheerful, because she **got through** her driving test this morning.
The plan to send an expedition **fell through**, owing to lack of money.
The day before we were due to leave, John tried **to back out of** going.
Come on, you said I could drive. You aren't going **to do me out of** my turn.
I'm sorry. I'm afraid we've **run out of** blue envelopes. You'll have to use a white one.
The two men **checked out of** the hotel and walked to the station.
Don't involve me in this argument. I intend to **keep out of** it.
I'm afraid the Americans have decided **to pull out of** the deal.

Now answer the following questions:

1 What might a traveller **check out of**?

2 If a politician made a statement and people immediately **saw through** it, what would the politician be doing?

3 Tom planned to take his mother and father to the theatre, but the visit **fell through**. Suggest a possible reason.

4 What might a hotel receptionist **put through**?

5 Mrs Jones had intended to make a cake, but she found that she had **run out of** sugar. What do you think she did?

6 Why do you think John suddenly tried to **back out of** being best man at George's wedding?

7 The workers went on strike because they felt they had been **done out of** something. Suggest what it might have been.

8 The young doctors had been studying for a long time. Now they were having a party and were obviously very happy. What do you think they had **got through**?

E Focus on grammar: modals

There are a number of words and expressions called **modals** which are used to express probability. They are useful and important, so need to be studied carefully.

Look at these examples from the reading text:

You **needn't** carry large amounts of cash with you . . . (ll. 4–5)
You **may** use your credit card in any Texas Superstores . . . (ll. 11–12)
You **might** wish to have a higher credit limit at some time. (ll. 22–3)

May/might can be used:

a	when giving or asking for permission.
Examples	Might I make some coffee?
	You may have the afternoon off.
b	to express the idea of 'perhaps'.
Examples	Susan may telephone this evening.
	Susan might telephone tomorrow.
	(**Might** suggests less probability than **may**.)

Must/have to are used to express obligation or duty.

Examples Your hair is too long. You must go to the barber.
All foreigners have to fill in one of these cards.
I had to fill in a card.

We use **had to** as the past of both **have to** and **must**.

Note that the negative form of **have to** is **do/does/did not have to**.

Mustn't/needn't mean different things.

Examples You mustn't smoke in this room. (It is forbidden to smoke.)
You needn't give me a receipt. (It isn't necessary to give me a receipt.)

Note also You don't have to go. (You have a choice as to whether to go or not.)

Should/ought to are used to remind someone of a moral responsibility, or to give advice or to recommend something.

Examples You ought to see that new film at the Odeon. (recommendation)
I think you should write to Laura. (moral responsibility)
You should see a doctor about your bad back. (advice)

Shouldn't/ought not to are the negative forms.

Examples You shouldn't make so much noise.
He ought not to behave like that.

F *Grammar practice*

Rewrite the following sentences using suitable modals in place of the phrases in **bold** *type.*

1 Visitors **are forbidden to** take photographs inside the castle.

2 You **are advised not to** drink the water without boiling it first.

3 I'm afraid I haven't got any change, but **it's possible that you will** get some at the newsagent's.

4 **It isn't necessary for you to** buy a return ticket, because I'll give you a lift back.

5 All members of the crew **are ordered to** report to their posts immediately.

6 She **has no choice but to** tell the police what she saw.

7 **There is a chance that** he **will** sell his house and buy a smaller one.

8 I think you **have a moral responsibility to** lend him the money.

G *Grammar practice*

Complete the following sentences using **might**, **must**, **mustn't**, **needn't** *or* **ought to**.

Example Mr Francis said to Miss Thomas: 'It's going to rain, so you **ought to take your umbrella**.'

1 When you travel to another country, the immigration officer always inspects your passport. So when you travel abroad, you . . .

2 I'm not sure where we are going for our holiday, but we . . .

3 Sudden sharp pains across the chest could indicate heart trouble. So if *you* get pains across your chest, you . . .

4 If you are driving your car towards some traffic lights and they turn red, you . . .

5 When the 'No smoking' sign lights up in the aircraft, it means that you . . .

6 I have already heard the story twice, so you . . .

7 When you visit a zoo, you often see the sign 'Do not feed the animals'. This means that you . . .

8 The doctor didn't know for certain what was wrong with Alfred, but he thought it . . .

H Focus on grammar: future simple

1   The future simple is often used to provide information about future happenings in a formal way, as in the following examples from the reading text:

The information . . . **will be treated** as strictly confidential. (ll. 30–31)
You **will** never **have to pay** a deposit . . . (l. 8)
You **won't pay** anything until . . . (l. 14)

Each statement is, in its way, a promise.

2   The future simple is also used in order to offer a solution to a problem.

For example

Susan Oh dear. I've forgotten my purse.
Anne Don't worry. **I'll lend** you some money.

Peter I don't know what time the train leaves.
George **I'll ring** the station and find out.

I Grammar practice

In the next few days some famous people will carry out official visits.

Look at the two lists below and decide

a   who will visit what.
b   what each person will do during the visit.

The people		The places	
1	The Queen of England	a	A Swedish gaol for young offenders
2	The President of the U.S.A.	b	The site of the next Olympic Games
3	A famous Hollywood film star	c	An agricultural college in Wales
4	The Secretary of the Society for Prison Reform	d	A Commonwealth conference in New Delhi
5	A famous heart surgeon	e	American troops based in Europe
6	The Archbishop of York	f	A medical conference in Toronto, Canada
7	The President of the World Athletics Association	g	A village church in the north of England
8	The Secretary of the National Farmers' Union	h	A film festival in the south of France

J *Focus on grammar:* 'going to' future; present continuous as a future tense

There are two other common ways of expressing the future in English:

1 'going to'

Examples   *Railway official to people on platform:* Stand back, please. The train**'s** just **going to leave**.
George to a friend: What **are** you **going to do** this afternoon?
Little boy: When I grow up, **I'm going to be** a pop musician.

The 'going to' future is used to express intentions, particularly when they are accompanied by strong emotions such as enthusiasm or anger. However, the speaker is often aware that what he is talking about may never happen.

2 the present continuous

Examples   The new store**'s opening** next week.
We**'re buying** the tickets tomorrow.
Paul **isn't taking** that job with the insurance company.

When the present continuous is used to express a future idea, the implication is that the event definitely will (or will not) take place.

K *Grammar practice*

You are having a conversation in a restaurant.
Choose the best future tense for each of the ten situations. Indicate where alternatives are acceptable.

1 You're in the restaurant. You look at the menu and decide to have steak and salad. Tell the waiter.

  a I'll have
  b I'm going to have } steak and salad.
  c I'm having

2 You are joined by a friend. You are still waiting for your meal. Tell your friend what you chose.

  a I'll have
  b I'm going to have } steak and salad.
  c I'm having

3 Offer to buy the wine.

  a I'll buy
  b I'm going to buy } the wine.
  c I'm buying

4   You have bought tickets for a holiday in Spain. Tell your friend about your plans.

   a We'll go
   b We're going to go } to Spain.
   c We're going

5   You have been invited to a rather formal dance. You have to take a partner. Tell your friend you have decided to take Pat.

   a I'll take
   b I'm going to take } Pat.
   c I'm taking

6   Your young brother has been having problems at school. You have decided to make an appointment to see the headmaster. Tell your friend.

   a I'll see
   b I'm going to see } the headmaster.
   c I'm seeing

7   Your friend Sheila is due to take her driving test next Tuesday. Tell your friend.

   a Sheila will take
   b Sheila is going to take } her driving test on Tuesday.
   c Sheila is taking

8   You show your friend some photographs you took. They aren't good and you have decided to buy a new camera. Tell your friend.

   a I'll buy
   b I'm going to buy } a new camera.
   c I'm buying

9   Your friend has to go to the station. You decide to give him/her a lift. Tell your friend.

   a I'll give
   b I'm going to give } you a lift to the station.
   c I'm giving

10 Your friend will be back at the weekend. Arrange to telephone him/her on Saturday morning.

   a I'll ring
   b I'm going to ring } you on Saturday morning.
   c I'm ringing

L Writing activity

Below and on page 48 are details of three customers who have applied for a Texas Superstores credit card. Imagine you work for Texas and have to decide whether or not these applicants should be given credit cards and what credit limit to allow them. Make your recommendations on page 49, giving reasons in the space provided. Do not write more than 50 words about each applicant.

TEXAS SUPERSTORES

Credit Account Application Form

Name and address: Mr. ☐ Mrs ☑ Miss ☐ Ms ☐

Name: *Martha WHITE*

Address: *4, HARLINGTON COURT*
BRIGHTON ROAD
HASTINGS

Years at this address: *27* Are you owner ☐ tenant ☑ with

parents ☐

Date of birth *4/1/20* single ☐ married ☐ divorced ☐ widow ☑

Employer: —

Business address: —

Present position: — *(pension)*

Years with this employer: — Total salary last year: *£1560*

Your bank: *I have a Post Office account*

Address of branch:

Account number: *372 521 788*

I would like a spending limit of: £100 ☐ £250 ☐ £500 ☑

Your signature: *Martha White*

Name and address: Mr ☑ Mrs ☐ Miss ☐ Ms ☐

Name: TOM PARKER

Address: 6 HANOVER SQUARE HASTINGS

Years at this address: 12 Are you owner ☐ tenant ☐ with parents ☑

Date of birth 10/6/66 single ☑ married ☐ divorced ☐ widow ☐

Employer: AT PRESENT UNEMPLOYED

Business address: —

Present position: — (Temporary Summer Work)

Years with this employer: Total salary last year: £560.

Your bank: Midland Bank

Address of branch: White Rock Branch (Hastings)

Account number: 2147 4088

I would like a spending limit of: £100 ☑ £250 ☐ £500 ☐

Your signature: T. Parker

Name and address: Mr ☐ Mrs ☐ Miss ☐ Ms ☑

Name: NICOLA PYM

Address: 24, FISHERMAN'S WALK HASTINGS

Years at this address: 6 Are you owner ☑ tenant ☐ with parents ☐

Date of birth 6/7/55 single ☑ married ☐ divorced ☐ widow ☐

Employer: PARKER AND JUDD, SOLICITORS

Business address: 10, White Rock Place, Hastings

Present position: SECRETARY

Years with this employer: 9 Total salary last year: £9,500 (approx.)

Your bank: Barclays Bank

Address of branch: Seaside, Hastings

Account number: 4022 5656

I would like a spending limit of: £100 ☐ £250 ☑ £500 ☐

Your signature: Nicola Pym

Name: **Martha White** .... Requested credit limit: ....

I recommend that this customer should/should not be issued with a credit card.

Remarks:

Name: **Tom Parker** .... Requested credit limit: ....

I recommend that this customer should/should not be issued with a credit card.

Remarks:

Name: **Nicola Pym** .... Requested credit limit: ....

I recommend that this customer should/should not be issued with a credit card.

Remarks:

●● M *Listening comprehension*

The scene is an airport in the United Kingdom. Listen carefully to the various announcements made over the loudspeakers, then decide whether the following statements are true or false and put a tick (√) in the appropriate box.

		True	False
1	The Gulf Air passengers are going to have a free meal before they board their plane to Muscat.		
2	Flight BC2724 has just arrived from New York.		
3	Lufthansa flight LH2301 is going to arrive late.		
4	The driver of the blue Mercedes must move his car as soon as possible.		
5	The West Ham United football team are going to travel somewhere by Pan American Airways.		
6	The three-year-old child cannot speak.		
7	Swissair flight SR1606 will leave later than planned.		
8	Passengers are advised to keep their luggage with them in case someone tries to steal it.		

For questions 9 and 10, write the names of the two lost children referred to in the final announcement.

9 ....

10 ....

●● N *Communicative practice:* preferences

Which would you prefer, — or — ? Would you rather do — or — ? Where would you rather go, to — or to — ?	I'd really prefer — I think I'd rather — If you don't mind, I'd like —

Model conversations

1 a Which would you prefer, ice cream or chocolate pudding?

b If you don't mind, I'd like chocolate pudding.

Work in pairs. Use the phrases in the box to make similar conversations, choosing one from X and one from Y.

X	Y
sausages and chips	egg and chips
hot chocolate	coffee
strawberry ice cream	vanilla ice cream

2 a Would you rather have tea or coffee?

b I'd really prefer tea, if you don't mind.

Continue working in pairs, using the phrases from X and Y.

3 a Where would you rather go, to the Pizza Palace or to the Indian restaurant?

b I think I'd rather go to the Indian restaurant.

Continue working in pairs. Use the phrases in the box to make similar conversations, choosing one from M and one from N.

M	N
the pictures the museum the swimming pool	the concert the art gallery the beach

Think of additional phrases like those in X and Y or M and N of your own and continue the practice.

◗◗ O Dialogue

Listen to the dialogue on page 52 twice, without looking at it. Then answer questions 1–6.

1 Does Eric prefer the old coffee or the new coffee?

2 What is *Banana Boat*?

3 Will viewers see the Benny Hartman show at the same time as it is being performed? Why/why not?

4 Would Pamela rather go to the cinema or to the television studio?

5 What do you think might be the reasons for Pamela's choice?

6 How do you think Eric feels about going to the television studio rather than seeing the film?

It's Sunday afternoon. Eric and Pamela have just eaten their Sunday lunch. Now they are sitting in the garden, drinking coffee.

Pam   What do you think of this coffee?

Eric   It's all right. Why? Is it a new sort?

Pam   Yes. I thought we'd try it for a change.

Eric   Mmh. It doesn't seem very different from the other sort to me.

5   *Pam*   Do you prefer the other sort?

Eric   No, not really. This seems O.K. By the way, do you want to go out this week? There's a new film on at the Granada called *Banana Boat*. It's supposed to be quite funny.

Pam   Oh, I forgot to tell you. Bridget phoned. She's offered to get us tickets for
10   the Benny Hartman show on Wednesday.

Eric   Bridget . . .?

Pam   You know . . . my friend who works for ABC television.

Eric   Do you like Benny Hartman?

Pam   I'm not mad about him, but I thought it would be fun to take part in a
15   television programme.

Eric   It's not live, is it?

Pam   No, it's filmed on video. But I thought it would be interesting to be there and then watch the programme at home later. See what bits they cut out.

Eric   Would you rather go there than to the cinema?

20   *Pam*   Oh, yes. I think it'd be nice.

Eric   All right then. We can see the film another time. When does the recording start?

Pam   Six o'clock. So you'll have to go to the studio straight from the office and I'll meet you there.

25   *Eric*   O.K.

Sometimes people say one thing and mean something a little different. For instance:

7 When Pam says, 'Yes. I thought we'd try it for a change.' (l. 3), does she mean:
a I thought we could find a better sort of coffee.
b I got tired of buying the other sort.

8 When Eric says, 'No, not really.' (l. 6), does he mean:
a I really prefer the other sort.
b I'd rather have this sort.
c I'm bored with the subject of coffee.

9 When Eric says, 'There's a new film . . . supposed to be quite funny. (ll.7–8), does he mean:
a Would you like to see it?
b I want to see it.

10 When Pam says, 'She's offered to get us tickets for the Benny Hartman show' (ll. 9–10), does she mean:
a I want to go
b Would you like to go?

Now look at one or two more things that Pam and Eric said and see if you can suggest the real meaning of each.

11 Eric: 'Do you like Benny Hartman?' (l. 13)

12 Pam: 'I'm not mad about him.' (l. 14)

13 Pam: 'I thought it would be interesting to be there and then watch the programme at home later.' (ll. 17–18)

14 Eric: 'Would you rather go there than to the cinema?' (l. 19)

P Writing activity

It is 4 o'clock in the afternoon. You are at home and you plan to stay in on your own this evening.

A young man knocks at the door and hands you a copy of the television programmes to be shown on Channels 1 and 2 this evening. He is carrying out audience research and you agree to answer his three questions:

1 'Can you tell me which programmes you will definitely watch this evening, and why?'

2 'Can you say which programmes you might watch, and why?'

3 'Which programmes will you definitely not watch, and why?'

Study the programmes on the two television channels, then write what you will tell the interviewer. You will need approximately 50 words to answer each question.

Television tonight:

Channel 1	Channel 2
7.00 The News	**7.00** Wonder Woman Linda Carter fights evil.
7.15 The World of Nature Swans	**7.30** The Price is Right Panel game
7.45 International Volleyball Cuba v South Korea	**8.00** Dallas The serial in which everyone owns an oil well
8.15 Long Night in the City Film: Charles Bronson, Lee Marvin	**8.30** The Business Programme The strong dollar and world trade
9.30 Frank Sinatra in Las Vegas Music, song, dance	**9.00** The News
10.00 Last Train out of Laramie Film: Western with Kirk Douglas	**9.15** News Review A look behind the headlines
11.30 Return of Frankenstein Film: Late night horror (1958)	**9.30** Carmen Shortened film version of the opera
1.00 Close down	**10.30** Computers are Friendly Aimed at those who think they're not.
	11.00 Time for Music Late night chamber music: Bach, Haydn, Mozart
	12.00 Close down

Unit 5   Bedtime

A Reading comprehension

Study the following words and phrases before you read the text.

friction disagreement
dead tired very, very tired
the evil moment the awful moment
to dread to fear
affluent rich
less prosperous less wealthy

to take something for granted to assume that this is what always happens
soothing comforting
a ritual a regular pattern of behaviour
sucking their thumb putting the thumb in the mouth
cuddling holding tightly

Read the text quickly and find the answers to these questions:

1   Why are children sometimes frightened when they are put to bed and the light is turned out?

2   Why do the children of very poor parents not usually suffer in the same way?

3   Who is Dr Spock?

Bedtime

Getting the children to bed can easily become the cause of friction in a family, for a child, although dead tired, will employ the most convincing and original arguments to put off the evil moment when the light is turned out and his parents leave him on his own. It is likely that it is not sleep itself that the
5   child dreads, but rather the dreams that accompany it. This is not really surprising. If a child goes to sleep one night and dreams that there is a crocodile in his bed, he will probably not be very keen to go to bed the following night.

In our affluent society children are often separated from their parents and
10   expected to sleep in a room of their own at a very early age. If this happens, a sensitive child will often suffer and he will express his fear and loneliness by crying and causing scenes at bedtime. It is interesting to note that in less prosperous societies children are in this respect more fortunate, for lack of space generally ensures that the whole family sleeps in one room. Frequently
15   several children share the same bed. So the child who objects to being left to sleep alone, or who insists on having the bedroom door left open, or a light left on, is merely showing an instinct for comfort and protection that many other children take for granted.

At a very early age most young children establish some kind of personal
20   ritual which they regularly perform as they relax and fall asleep, sucking their thumb, rolling a corner of the sheet between their fingers, or cuddling a favourite doll or teddy bear. Dr Spock, the author of a number of well-known books on the art of bringing up children, advises parents that such bedtime rituals can be deliberately encouraged, until they become soothing
25   habits which help to calm the child's fears.

Adults, too, often go through some ritual performance before they go to bed – they clean their teeth, drink a cup of tea, take the dog for a walk, or bolt all the doors. If you ask someone to say exactly why he does such things night after night, he will find it difficult to explain, but if, for some reason, he is
30 prevented from following his normal routine, he will probably find it very hard indeed to get to sleep.

Now read the text carefully and answer the following:

4 What happens at bedtime if children are afraid to be left alone in the dark?

5 What sort of children are most likely to be affected by such fears?

6 Give examples of things small children might do as they go to sleep.

7 What advice does Dr Spock give to parents having problems with their children at bedtime?

8 In what circumstances might adults find it difficult to get to sleep?

B *Multiple choice questions*

Choose the best answer.

1 One should not be astonished

a if children always dream about crocodiles.
b if children are often frightened by their dreams.
c if children always argue with their parents.
d if children often want the light on in their beds.

2 The children of poor parents

a object to sleeping by themselves.
b sleep in the same room as their parents
c sometimes sleep in the same room as their brothers and sisters.
d never sleep alone.

3 Most very young children

a follow the same routine every time they go to sleep.
b put a finger in their mouth as they go to sleep.
c hold on to the sheet as they go to sleep.
d like to have a doll or teddy bear with them as they go to sleep.

4 Dr Spock

a has written some famous books.
b has written a number of books about art.
c has written books about sick children.
d has written books advising people how to become parents.

5 Grown-ups might find it difficult to get to sleep

a if they forgot to clean their teeth before going to bed.
b if they didn't remember to lock the doors before going to bed.
c if they were forced to change their usual pattern of behaviour before going to bed.
d if they were asked to explain why they did certain things before going to bed.

C Word study

Indicate the words and phrases which could be used to complete each sentence. Note that there may be more than one acceptable answer.

1 I .... the policeman to the police station.

a accompanied **b** followed **c** went **d** walked **e** told

2 The new taxes caused great .... among the poorer people.

a pain **b** pains **c** misery **d** suffering **e** hardship

3 Her doctor .... her change her job.

a persuaded **b** encouraged **c** advised **d** ordered **e** made

4 'I am looking for ....,' said the man.

a employment **b** an employment **c** a job **d** a work **e** work

5 The two younger children were .... by their elder sister, Felicity.

a brought up **b** brought back **c** brought round **d** brought in **e** brought over

6 The .... of the accident has never been established.

a reason **b** cause **c** purpose **d** result **e** explanation

7 Please wear your badge at all times. This will .... that you are recognized immediately by our security staff.

a ensure **b** insure **c** prove **d** establish **e** guarantee

8 The cottage was very small and the family complained about the lack of ....

a place **b** room **c** rooms **d** space **e** spaces

D Word study

If a child dreads going to sleep because he is afraid he might have nightmares (bad dreams), then obviously his dreams are **frightening**. Films, too, can be frightening for a small child because he is unable to separate fantasy from reality.

Here are some more adjectives we might use when talking about films:

dull	**moving**
extraordinary	**ridiculous**
fascinating	**strange**
foreign	**terrific**
humorous	**terrifying**
memorable	**violent**

Write each adjective from the list above next to its meaning:

1 very frightening: ....
2 containing scenes of brutality: ....
3 likely to make people laugh: ....
4 very, very good: ....
5 unusual: ....
6 most unusual: ....
7 made abroad: ....
8 likely to affect people emotionally: ....
9 very silly: ....
10 boring: ....
11 very, very interesting: ....
12 unforgettable: ....

Work in pairs. Decide which of the adjectives above might be useful in a discussion about any two of the following types of film:

a a comedy   **c** a science fiction film   **e** a documentary film
b a cowboy film   **d** a film about nature

Now compare your answers with those of another pair of students.

E Focus on grammar: first conditional

Look at these sentences from the reading text:

If a child . . . dreams that there is a crocodile in his bed, **he will . . . not be** very keen to go to bed the following night. (ll.6–8)

If this happens, a sensitive child **will often suffer** . . . (ll. 10–11)

If you ask someone to say . . . why he does such things . . ., **he will find** it difficult to explain . . . (ll. 28–29)

In this type of conditional sentence, **if** is followed by the present simple tense and the main clause is in a future tense, usually the future simple. Either or both clauses can be negative. We use the first conditional when we are talking about two events, one of which is a natural consequence of the other.

If I feel better tomorrow (but I may not), **I will come** to work. (The implication is that, if I **don't** feel better, I **won't** come to work.)

F Grammar practice

Henry is cold. The electric fire is off.
If he (Henry) turns on the fire, he will soon get (be) warm.

Comment on the following situations in the same way.

1 Henry can't see. The light is off.

2 The car won't start. There is no petrol in the tank.

3 Sally has a bad tooth. The dentist pulls out bad teeth.

4 The washing is on the line. It's nearly dry, but it looks as if it's going to rain.

5 When he watches horror movies, Harold has bad dreams. There's a horror movie on the TV tonight.

6 Susan never knows what time the trains leave. A timetable contains this information.

7 Don't touch that dog. He bites strangers.

8 Tom must be in London by 2 o'clock. The journey takes an hour and there is a train that leaves at 12.45.

9 Milly suffers from travel sickness. She can't decide whether to take her pills. They make her sleepy.

10 Peter is going to park his car on a yellow line. People who park on yellow lines get a parking ticket.

G Focus on grammar: *unless* in first conditional sentences

Note that **unless**+affirmative is often used as an alternative to **if**+negative.

Examples   If I don't take a sleeping pill, I won't be able to sleep.
Unless I take a sleeping pill, I won't be able to sleep.

We'll go for a picnic tomorrow, if it doesn't rain.
We'll go for a picnic tomorrow, unless it rains.

H Grammar practice

Complete each of the following sentences in such a way that it means exactly the same as the sentence before it:

1   If I don't see you at the station, I'll ask for you at the hotel.
Unless I . . .

2   They won't win unless they play better than they did last week.
If they . . .

3   The plane won't be able to land if the weather doesn't improve.
Unless . . .

4   He'll never find a job unless he has a haircut.
If he . . .

5   They won't allow him on the ship unless he's got his passport.
If he . . .

6   He won't be able to help you if you don't tell him the truth.
Unless . . .

7   He won't lose weight unless he eats less.
If he . . .

8   Unless you write to him and apologize, he won't forgive you.
If you . . .

9   She'll have to sell the house unless she gets another job.
If she . . .

10   If I can't get it repaired, I'll have to buy a new one.
Unless I . . .

I Focus on grammar: gerunds

A gerund always ends in –ing. It frequently appears as the subject of a sentence.

Examples **Getting the children to bed** can . . . become the cause of friction . . . (l. 1)
Jogging is good for you.

Gerunds are also often used after certain verbs and expressions.

Examples So the child **who objects to being** left to sleep alone, or **who insists on having** the bedroom door left open . . . (ll. 15–16)

. . . but if . . .**he is prevented from following** his normal routine . . . (ll. 29–30)

Here is a short list of useful verbs and expressions which are often followed by a gerund:

admit to, apologize for, avoid, can't help, can't stand, delay, deny, dislike, don't mind, dread, enjoy, excuse, fancy, finish, forgive, hate, imagine, insist on, keep, like, look forward to, love, prefer, prevent, risk, stop, suggest, understand, worth, would you mind?

Examples **I apologize for waking** you so early.
We can't imagine living there.
They are looking forward to seeing you again.
It's worth seeing that film.
Would you mind posting this letter for me?

Notice that these expressions can also be followed by a noun or a pronoun:

He apologized for his sister's behaviour.
She risked her life to save the child.
Will you excuse me?

J Grammar practice

Complete sentences 1–12, like this:

There is at least one job that every housewife dislikes, and Hilda
hated . . . (washing the dishes)

1 Different people enjoy themselves in different ways and Lilian enjoyed . . .

2 The detective wasn't sure that Fraser had any information, but he thought it was worth . . .

3 Nurse Rogers had no objection to taking someone's temperature, but she disliked . . .

4 Life is very miserable if one has nothing to look forward to and Hector was looking forward to . . .

5 The boys insisted that they had not eaten the chicken, but they admitted . . .

6 Without a driving licence Briggs would have been unable to do his job, yet he risked . . .

7   Mr Hall was not a friendly man. Although he saw his neighbours every day, he always tried to avoid . . .

8   Steven felt cold and tired. He certainly didn't fancy . . .

9   Jenkins was accused of the theft, but he denied . . .

10 Mary wasn't at all keen on cooking, but she didn't mind . . .

11 The man who had been knocked down said he felt all right, but the doctor insisted on . . .

12 Thomas didn't like going to see the doctor, but he absolutely dreaded . . .

K Listening comprehension

You are going to hear an extract from a radio interview about children suffering from dyslexia, a condition which affects the ability to learn to read and write. You will hear the interview twice. Listen carefully, then answer the questions.

For questions 1 and 2 write in the missing word:

1   Dr Storey is the chairman of a special educational .... group.

2   Dyslexic children have problems in the more complicated communicative ....

	True	False
For questions 3–12 tick (√) whether you think the statements are true or false:		
3 Teachers often have more than thirty children in their class.		
4 Dyslexic children often do less well at school than they should.		
5 Teachers find it easy to discover that a child is dyslexic.		
6 Duncan Goodhew is a well-known sporting personality.		
7 Susan Hampshire is a famous actor.		
8 Children suffering from dyslexia don't find it easy to learn to spell.		
9 If dyslexia is discovered early enough it can be completely cured.		
10 The new courses will last for a week.		
11 These courses will be open to parents and teachers.		
12 Parents who think their child is dyslexic should tell the child's teacher.		

L Writing activity

Work in pairs. Make a list of the advantages of being able to read and write and the disadvantages of not being able to.

Now work individually. Young people who are unable to read or write sometimes become involved in crime at a very early age – at fourteen, fifteen or sixteen years old. Imagine that you are the director of a special course aimed at teaching youngsters with this problem to read and write.

It is the first day of the course and you decide to give a short talk to the new arrivals. You are going to start by warning the young people how difficult life will be if they don't learn to read and write. Then you are going to explain how the course will help them.

Write the speech you will make. Use 120–180 words.

M Interview

1   *Work in groups of three or four. Look at the photograph on page 63, then ask and answer these questions:*

a   Where do you think it was taken?
b   What can you say about the aeroplane?
c   Who do you think the man is? What is he doing?
d   What do you think is going to happen?
e   Have you ever flown in an aeroplane?
f   Were you scared?
g   Tell the other people in your group about your first flight.

2   *Read the passage silently, then answer the questions below.*

Yes, I can understand that in the circumstances you want to get home as soon as possible. You're quite correct. There's a flight leaving for New York this evening; but you must appreciate that this is a very busy time of the year. At the moment that flight is fully booked and we shall only be able to find you a seat if there's a last-minute cancellation.

a   Who is speaking?
b   Who is that person speaking to?
c   Do you think the two speakers can see one another?
d   What does the person being spoken to want?
e   Suggest what the circumstances might be.
f   Do you think the person being spoken to is going to be lucky or not? Explain why.

3   Airlines have been experiencing difficulty over security recently. *Discuss these difficulties.*

4   What steps do airlines take to combat the threat of terrorism? *Suggest further measures they might take.*

N Writing activity

Think of some of the remarkable discoveries and inventions that have changed all our lives. What effect(s) have they had?
Here is a short list to start you off: the wheel, the steam engine, gunpowder.

Now choose an invention or discovery and write 120–160 words on 'A discovery that has changed our lives' *or* 'An invention that has changed our lives'.

In your first paragraph say what life was like *before* the discovery/invention. In your middle paragraph(s) describe the changes that resulted. In your final paragraph say whether you would have preferred to have lived before rather than after the discovery/invention in question.

Unit 6   *The Venus Fly Trap*

A *Reading comprehension*

Study the following words and phrases before you read the text.

Dionaea muscipula the Latin name of a plant
heart centre
whiskery with whiskers, the long hairs that grow beside a cat's mouth
luscious rich and attractive
fly an insect
thrilled very excited, very pleased
chiffon fine, transparent material, often used for making evening dresses
to buck you up to cheer you up and make you feel more lively
the States the United States of America

Read the text quickly and find the answers to these questions:

1 What is 'different' about the Venus Fly Trap?

2 Does the plant belong to Merle or Daphne?

3 Where do Daphne's children live?

The Venus Fly Trap

'What's the matter?'

'That plant, Merle, it moved.'

'That's because you touched it. When you touch one of its mouths it closes up. It's called Dionaea muscipula.'

5 The plant stood alone in an earthenware pot contained in an elaborate white stand. It looked very healthy. It had delicate shiny leaves and from its heart grew five red-gold blossoms. As Daphne peered more closely she saw that these resembled mouths, as Merle had put it, far more than flowers, whiskery mouths, soft and ripe and luscious. One of these was now closed.

10 'Doesn't it have a common name?'

'Of course it does. The Venus Fly Trap. Muscipula means fly-eater, dear.'

'Whatever do you mean?'

'It eats flies. I've been trying to grow one for years. I was absolutely thrilled when I succeeded.'

15 'Yes, but what do you mean, it eats flies? It's not an animal.'

'It is in a way, dear. The trouble is there aren't many flies here. I feed it on little bits of meat. You've gone rather pale, Daphne. Have you got a head-ache? We'll have our sherry now and then I'll see if I can catch a fly and you can see it eat it up.'

20 'I'd really much rather not, Merle,' said Daphne, backing away from the plant. 'I don't want to hurt your feelings but I don't – well, I hate the idea of catching free live things and feeding them to – to that.'

'Free live things? We're talking about flies.' Merle, large and perfumed, grabbed Daphne's arm and pulled her away. Her dress was of red chiffon
25 with trailing sleeves and her fingernails matched it. 'The trouble with you,' said Merle, 'is that you're a mass of nerves and you're much worse now than you were when we were girls. I thank God every day of my life I don't know what it is to be neurotic. Here you are, your sherry. I've put it in a big glass to buck you up. I'm going to make it my business to look after you, Daphne.
30 You don't know anybody else in London, do you?'

'Hardly anybody,' said Daphne, sitting down where she couldn't see the Venus Fly Trap. 'My boys are in the States and my daughter's in Scotland.'

'Well, you must come up here every day. You won't be intruding. When I first knew you were definitely coming I said to myself, I'm going to see to it Daphne isn't lonely.'

From *The Venus Fly Trap* by Ruth Rendell

Now read the text carefully and answer the following:

4 What caused the plant to move?

5 Why did Daphne go pale?

6 What does Merle imply when she says: 'Free live things?'

7 Describe Merle and the clothes she is wearing.

8 Why did Merle put the sherry in a large glass?

9 What influenced Daphne in her choice of seat?

10 How do you know that Daphne hasn't been living in London for long?

B Multiple choice questions

Choose the best answer.

1 a The plant moved because Merle touched it.
  b The plant moved because one of the mouths closed.
  c The plant moved because Daphne came into contact with it.
  d The plant moved because a fly touched one of the mouths.

2 Merle was terribly excited when she was able

  a to give the Venus Fly Trap a piece of meat.
  b to feed the Venus Fly Trap on flies.
  c to grow a Venus Fly Trap.
  d to plant a Venus Fly Trap.

3 Daphne went pale

  a because she had got a headache.
  b because she thought Merle was going to give the plant a fly.
  c at the thought of giving the plant a piece of meat.
  d at the thought of the plant eating a living creature.

4 a Merle was wearing a red, cotton dress.
  b Merle had red fingernails.
  c Merle was rather a nervous person.
  d Merle's dress had tight sleeves.

5 a Daphne had a son who lived in America.
  b Daphne didn't know anyone in London except Merle.
  c Daphne came to visit Merle every day.
  d Daphne chose a seat from where she could watch the plant.

C Word study

Look at this sentence from the text:

As Daphne **peered** more closely she saw that these [blossoms] resembled mouths. (ll. 7–8)

to peer at: to look at very closely

On the next page are some verbs we use to describe different ways of looking at things:

to catch a glimpse of	**to peep at**	**to observe**
to glare at	**to watch**	**to glance at**
to study	**to gaze at**	**to stare at**
to examine	**to search for**	**to survey**

Match the verbs above with the definitions below:

1 to take a quick look at:

2 to look at something very hard with your eyes open wide, often in surprise:

3 to look at a moving object:

4 to see and to notice:

5 to see something for a brief instant, but not very clearly:

6 to look at something very hard, often with admiration:

7 to look at somebody or something very angrily:

8 to look at something very carefully, taking in all the detail:

9 to look at something rather quickly and nervously, as if not wanting to be noticed:

10 to look for:

11 to look at something very carefully, as if looking for clues:

12 to look over a wide area (often from a raised position):

Work in pairs and decide which of the verbs above might be used to replace **see** *or* **look** (**at**) *in the situations below. There will sometimes be more than one acceptable answer.*

1 Tom kicked the ball high into the air and it disappeared over the wall. A moment later there was the sound of breaking glass. Tom's heart sank and he **looked** (1) nervously over the wall and found himself **looking** (2) straight into the eyes of Mr Henderson, who had been **looking at** (3) the daffodils in his garden. Mr Henderson **looked at** (4) him. 'You'll have to pay for that,' he said angrily.

2 The train stopped at a small station and a young woman got into the carriage. She **looked** briefly **at** (5) Charles and sat down in the far corner. The train started again and the young woman **looked** (6) out of the window, lost in her private thoughts. Charles **looked at** (7) her secretly from behind his newspaper.

3 The detective paused at the kitchen window and **looked at** (8) the yard outside. Then he turned his attention to the window itself. He **looked at** (9) the window sill carefully and he **saw** (10) exactly where the broken glass had fallen.
'I suppose you're **looking for** (11) clues,' said Mr Rose, eagerly.
The detective **looked at** (12) him. 'You're sure nothing's been touched?' he enquired.
'Certainly not,' replied Mr Rose, shaking his head vigorously.

D Word study

Daphne says: 'My boys are in the States and my daughter's in Scotland.' (l. 32)

We can only guess what happened to Daphne's husband, but we know that she has been married and has **brought up** at least three children.

The word **up** is often used in the formation of phrasal verbs. *Look at these examples:*

Why didn't you **back me up** when I complained about the heating?

After their mother died, the two daughters were **brought up** by their aunt.

Prost finally **caught up with** Shenton on the forty-ninth lap.

The lawyers will **draw up** a new contract for you to sign.

When I asked about the money he **hung up** on me.

The train was **held up** for two hours because of the snow.

I've **looked** that expression **up** in two dictionaries, but I can't find it.

The police car **pulled up** in front of the bank.

I'm not going to **put up with** this inconvenience any longer.

She **set up** a new record for the women's 100 metres last week.

After he was sacked from the oil corporation, he **took up** farming.

The stolen painting **turned up** six years later at a country sale.

*Use a suitable phrasal verb from the examples above in place of the words in **bold** in the following sentences:*

1   I'm sorry I'm late. I was **delayed** by the traffic.

2   I've **tolerated** your rudeness long enough. I think you'd better find somewhere else to live.

3   Uncle Charles **appeared unexpectedly** at Samantha's wedding.

4   The ambulance **stopped** outside the hospital.

5   The finance minister has **designed** a new plan to combat the problem of inflation.

6   Although he has lived in Paris for many years, he was **raised** in a small country town.

7   We rang the number given in the advertisement and asked to speak to Mr Archer, but as soon as we said we were from the B.B.C. he **put down the receiver**.

8   I told the boss I didn't think we were being paid enough, but nobody **supported** me.

9   After Thompson left the army, he **began to interest himself in** photography.

10 The stolen lorry was chased by two policemen on motor bikes and they finally **drew level with** it at the crossroads.

E *Focus on grammar:* present perfect simple; present perfect continuous

Look at these sentences from the text:

You've gone rather pale, Daphne. (l. 17)

Here you are, your sherry. **I've put** it in a big glass to buck you up. (ll. 28–29)

I've been trying to grow one for years. (l. 13)

The first two sentences use the present perfect simple and the last one uses the present perfect continuous.

We use the **present perfect simple**:

1   When describing a past event that took place at a *time* which is not stated or implied:

I've lost my scissors.
Gloria has sold her car.

2   When describing very recent events, often with the adverb **just**:

Tom has just telephoned.
I've just heard the news on the radio.

3   When we wish to indicate that an event which started in the past is still going on, using **for** with a **length of time** and **since** with a **point in time**.

They've lived there **for two years**. (They still live there.)
He's worked here **for three months**. (He still works here.)
That car has been there **since yesterday**. (It is still there.)
They've used that laboratory for medical experiments **since 1972**. (They are still using it for that purpose.)

Notice how the use of the past simple tense would alter the meaning of the last four sentences:

They lived there for two years. (They do not live there any more.)
He worked here for three months. (He does not work here now.)
That car was there yesterday. (Either it is no longer there or it is still there but has been moved in the meantime.)
They used that laboratory for medical experiments. (They do not use it for that purpose now.)

We use the **present perfect continuous**:

1   When we want to stress the continuity of the action or series of events we are describing, even if the action has now stopped:

It's been raining all night. (Look how wet the streets are.)
I've been cooking. (That's why I'm wearing this apron and that's why my face is so red.)

2 When we want to imply that the action, or the consequences of the action, will continue into the future:

They've been waiting at the airport since this morning. (They are still waiting and they still don't know when they will get away.)

We've been discussing the wedding. (There will probably be a lot more discussion of the subject.)

Sometimes it hardly matters whether we use the present perfect simple or the present perfect continuous.

Compare They've been living there for two years.
They've lived there for two years.

In other cases, however, we can make a clear distinction between the continuous action and an action that has been interrupted:

I've been ringing his number since 9 o'clock. (I've done nothing else.)
I've rung his number three times since 9 o'clock. (But I've done other things as well.)

She's been taking photographs all afternoon. (She's concentrated all her energies on this activity.)
She's taken a lot of photographs this afternoon. (But she's also chatted to people, eaten sandwiches and drunk tea.)

F *Grammar practice*

Work in groups of three or four.
Tell the other members of your group

1 of a place you've been to and another place you've never been to.
Example I've been to Moscow, but I've never been to Delhi.

2 of a sort of food you have eaten and another sort you've never eaten.

3 of a book you've read and another you've never read.

4 of a famous person you've admired for a long time.

5 how long you've lived in your present home.

6 how long you've had the shoes you're wearing.

Now tell your group

7 how long you've been studying English. (I've been studying . . .)

8 how long you've been living at your present address.

9 how long you've been smoking. (What tense will you use if you're a non-smoker?)

10 how long you've been driving. (Again, what tense will you use if you have no driving licence?)

G *Grammar practice*

Tony has spent the last five weeks with a film crew making a documentary film in North, Central and South America. Here is a letter he has written to his friend, Sheila, who lives in England.

Put the verbs in brackets into the past simple, present perfect simple or present perfect continuous.

                                        Mar del Plata
                                        Argentina
                                        8 November 19 –

Dear Sheila,
I am sitting in a comfortable chair, in a very comfortable
hotel in Mar del Plata, where we (film)[1] for the last three
days. From my window I can see the Atlantic Ocean.
     As you know we (leave)[2] England five weeks ago and (fly)[3]
to Canada, where we (take)[4] some marvellous shots of Eskimos,
polar bears and seals. Then we (spend)[5] a week in the French
part of Canada, before travelling on to the United States. We
(stay)[6] there for a fortnight and then (cross)[7] the border into
Mexico, where we (meet)[8] some charming people.
     After that we (go)[9] to Maracaibo, in Venezuela. My goodness,
it (be)[10] hot there. Then we (travel)[11] to Sao Paulo, in Brazil,
where we (interview)[12] a lot of interesting people. We (be)[13]
in Argentina for just over a week. I must say, wherever we (stay)[14]
people (be)[15] extraordinarily kind and hospitable. I (promise)[16]
to send so many postcards that I shall have to get myself a
secretary. Of course we (shoot)[17] far more film than we shall
be able to use. Pam and I (not have)[18] time to edit any of it
yet. You won't believe this, but we (work)[19] terribly hard,
although it (be)[20] great fun.
     If all goes well we shall be flying home at the end of next
week. I'll give you a ring when I get back.
     Love,

     Tony

H *Grammar practice*

Notice these three ways of expressing the same idea:

I last **saw** him three months ago.
I **haven't seen** him **for** three months.
It's three months **since** I **saw** him.

Finish each of the following sentences in such a way that it means the same as the previous sentence.

1   John hasn't visited the club for three months.
    It's . . .

2   I haven't drunk coffee like this for years.
    It's . . .

3   I last met Toby two years ago.
    I haven't . . .

4   It's two years since we went to the seaside.
    We last . . .

5   I last ate chocolate like this when we were in Switzerland.
    I haven't . . .

6   I last saw a doctor in 1984.
    I haven't . . .

7   It's nearly ten years since Charles appeared on the stage.
    Charles last . . .

8   Emma hasn't had one of those awful headaches for a long time.
    It's . . .

9   We last worked together seven years ago.
    We haven't . . .

10 I haven't heard that tune for years.
    It's . . .

●● I Listening comprehension

Listen to this radio interview with an expert on old gramophone
records. Then decide whether the following statements are true or false.

	True	False
1 78 rpm records go round seventy-eight times per second.		
2 78 rpm records are rather fragile.		
3 Sid would pay a very low price for the King George V record.		
4 The value of a record doesn't necessarily depend upon its age.		
5 45s are more likely to be valuable than 78s.		
6 Some hit records made in the sixties by David Bowie and Rod Stewart are worth a lot of money.		
7 Rock 'n' roll fans will always pay more for records than jazz fans.		
8 In order to fetch a high price, records must be in good condition.		

Now, taking your information from the interview, complete the following sentences:

9 78s are not usually worth a lot of money because . . .

10 Early jazz records do not usually fetch a big price because . . .

11 45s by Elvis Presley might fetch a good price provided that . . .

J Writing activity

Martin Cummins is interviewing record collector Edward Vincent on a radio
programme in which guests are invited to play some of their favourite records and
talk about them. *You are Martin Cummins. Ask Edward Vincent questions.*

1 *M.C.* . . .
  E.V. Well, I like a very wide range of music, actually.

2 *M.C.* . . .
  E.V. Oh, for many years. Since I was sixteen, in fact.

3 *M.C.* . . .
  E.V. I'm not sure what you mean by 'many'. I buy records from time to time, whenever something takes my fancy.

4 *M.C.* . . .
  E.V. It was a record of songs by Placido Domingo. I heard one of the songs on a radio programme and I liked it.

5 *M.C.* . . .
  E.V. No, I hardly ever buy tapes. I have a tape deck on my hi-fi system, but I very rarely use it.

6 *M.C.* . . .
  E.V. Well, I thought we'd start with something bright and tuneful. I'd like to play the overture to *Carmen*.

  M.C. Fine

K Interview

1 *Look at the photograph, then answer these questions:*

a What time of year is it? How do you know?

b What sort of problems and difficulties do you think the snow might cause
i in towns?
ii in the country?

c Do you ever get snow in your country?

d Can you think of any particular group of people who are unhappy to see snow? Why are they unhappy?

e What sort of people might be happy to see snow? Why?

f In certain countries snow falls every year and many people enjoy snow sports. How many winter sports can you think of? Have you ever taken part in any of these activities?

2   *Read the passage silently, then answer the questions below it:*

> A spokesman for the Central Famine Relief Agency warned today that thousands of people will die of starvation if food supplies are not sent immediately to parts of the Sudan. No rain has fallen during the last eight months and the crops have failed.

a   Decide if this is

an extract from a book on agriculture   an item of news
a paragraph from a political pamphlet   an advertisement

Would you expect to hear this or read it?
Explain why people's lives are in danger.

b   Do you think it is possible for such situations to be avoided?
Do the richer countries do enough to help their poorer neighbours?
What steps should we take to prevent such things happening in the future?

L Writing activity

Write 120–180 words on 'How snow and ice affect people's lives'.

In your first paragraph say how people's lives are affected by very cold weather. Then go on to talk about the difficulties caused by snow and ice. In your second paragraph mention the people who are pleased to see the snow and explain why they like the cold weather. In your final paragraph say how you feel personally.

Test 2

To be done without the aid of a dictionary.
No looking back to earlier sections of the book allowed.

Time	1 hour 15 minutes (plus the listening test)
Total possible marks	70
Ratings	50 marks or above **Good**
	38 marks or above **Fair**
	37 marks or below **Disappointing**. You are advised to spend some time revising Units 4–6.

 A *Listen to the telephone conversation, then fill in the missing items. You will hear the conversation twice:*

1 The woman is telephoning the ....

2 She wants to go to ....

3 She intends to leave about .... o'clock.

4 The slow train leaves at ....

5/6 There are fast trains leaving at .... and ....

7 The day return fare is £ ....

8 The monthly return fare is £ ....

9 The woman decides to catch the ....

10 She also decides to have .... on the train.

10 marks

B *Read the text then choose the best answers:*

It was still dark when the little party reached the beach. The general public was still tucked up in bed, so the promenade was deserted.

Hodge climbed out of the Land Rover and made his way across the pebbles to the water's edge. He stood for a moment, gazing dreamily out across the ocean to where the French coast lay. It was still hidden in darkness, although a pale strip of light on the horizon announced the coming of the dawn.

Thompson, the official time-keeper, was demanding coffee in his broad Scots accent.
'See to that, Douglas,' ordered O'Leary, 'there's a thermos behind the driving seat. I dare say Hodge could do with a drop – just half a cup. We don't want him to start with a lot of liquid inside him.'
'Is he allowed to drink on the way across?' asked Douglas.
'Of course he is and he can take a snack whenever he fancies one, but whatever happens he mustn't lay a finger on the boat. If he does it means instant disqualification.'

'Ten minutes to go,' announced O'Leary some time later. 'Come along, Frank. Let's get this grease on.'

Hodge removed his track suit and O'Leary began rubbing the thick grease all over his body.

'I suppose the grease provides some sort of protection,' remarked Douglas. Nobody replied.

Hodge felt as if he were somewhere else; an observer, watching the preparations. All the months of training, with O'Leary constantly at his side, all the time trials, were over. The moment had arrived. He had not slept well. He had dreamt that he swam on and on, till he could hear the sound of the surf breaking on the French shore and that huge waves had driven him back towards the English coast. In fact there was no breeze. The surface was like that of a mill pond.

'O.K.,' said the photographer from the *Daily Express*. 'Let's have a cheery smile.'

1   The promenade was deserted because

a   it was late at night.
b   it was early in the morning.
c   it was bedtime.
d   it was too dark to see.

2 a   Hodge looked at the French coast.
b   Hodge looked at the sea.
c   Hodge looked towards the French coast.
d   Hodge looked into the sea.

3 a   Hodge is going to swim the English Channel.
b   Hodge will swim the English Channel.
c   Hodge is swimming the English Channel.
d   Hodge hopes to swim the English Channel.

4   While he is swimming

a   Hodge can eat and drink.
b   Hodge can eat but not drink.
c   Hodge can drink but not eat.
d   Hodge can not eat or drink.

5 a   The sea was a bit rough.
b   The sea was very rough.
c   The sea was fairly calm.
d   The sea was extremely calm.

10 marks

C

*The word in **bold** type in the left-hand margin can be used to form a word that fits in the blank space in each sentence. Fill each space in this way:*

Example

foreigner   He has a ....*foreign*............ wife.

fascination 1 I heard a .... talk on the radio last night.

humour 2 P. G. Wodehouse wrote many .... stories.

prosperity 3 Duffy lives in a .... suburb of Sheffield.

memory 4 It certainly was a .... occasion.

month 5 We shall send you a .... bill.

agriculture 6 He is studying at an .... college in Norfolk.

excitement 7 It was a very .... race.

medicine 8 Her younger son is a .... student.

loneliness 9 He lives in a .... cottage on the coast.

aggression 10 The miner's leader made a very .... speech.

10 marks

D

Choose the word or phrase which best completes the sentence:

1 Her husband was killed in a train crash, so she had to bring .... three children on her own.
 a round **b** up **c** along **d** on

2 I want you to put .... a call to Dallas immediately.
 a through **b** up **c** over **d** in

3 Sorry we're late. We were held .... on the motorway because of an accident.
 a up **b** out **c** over **d** on

4 As soon as I asked who was speaking, he hung ....
 a on **b** out **c** up **d** in

5 I'd offer to make you some coffee, but I'm afraid we've run ....
 a up **b** out **c** through **d** on

5 marks

E   *Finish each of the following sentences in such a way that it means the same as the sentence before it:*

1   I haven't eaten this sort of cheese before.
     It's . . .

2   It's three years since Jack went to Australia.
     Jack . . .

3   I can't help you unless you tell me the whole story.
     If . . .

4   Dancing isn't allowed.
     You . . .

5   We first met three years ago.
     It's . . .

6   The party won't be any fun unless Robbie comes.
     If . . .

7   It's four years since Tom was in Paris.
     Tom hasn't . . .

8   It's not necessary to wash those dishes just now.
     You . . .

9   There is a chance of rain this afternoon.
     It . . .

10   It would be a very good idea if you saw the dentist.
     You . . .

20 marks

F   *Make all the changes and additions necessary to produce a letter of enquiry:*

Dear Mr Henderson,

1   I am / student / and I / like / come / your school / improve English.

2   I have / friend / who recommend / your school / me.

3   He / spend / three months / your school / last year / and learn / lot.

4   You / remember / student called / Mr Al Sylah?

5   I / study English / four years / my own country.

6   However / I believe / learn / lot more quickly / in England / I could here.

7   I want / take / First Certificate examination / next June.

8   You have / special class / students / who wish / take this exam?

I would be grateful if you could send me a copy of your prospectus.

Yours sincerely,

A. Al Bathani

15 marks
(2 marks for each sentence, except for number 7 which carries 1 mark)

Unit 7   *The Mildenhall Treasure*

A *Reading comprehension*

Study the following words and phrases before you read the text.

to plough a field to dig up a field before planting potatoes, etc.
soil earth
a crust a hard outer covering
a hoard a secret store
an archaeologist a person who studies history by digging up ancient buildings, tools, pottery etc.
a court hearing an inquiry into the facts, in front of a judge
a token payment a small payment made in recognition of some service that has been carried out

The Mildenhall Treasure

One bitterly cold afternoon in January 1942 a man by the name of Gordon Butcher was ploughing a field near Mildenhall in Suffolk when the plough struck an object buried in the earth. He immediately stopped the tractor, got off and went to see what the object was. Kneeling down, he dug the soil away
5   with his hands until suddenly he caught sight of a piece of green-coloured metal.

Although he was not a particularly well-educated man, Butcher knew that Romans had lived in this part of Britain and that Roman objects were sometimes found here. He also knew that a man called Ford, for whom he was
10   working, was interested in such objects, so he set off across the fields to tell him of his find.

Ford was mending a piece of farm machinery. 'What's up?' he asked.
'The plough hit a piece of metal,' said Butcher.
'What kind of metal?'
15   'I think it's a big plate,' replied Butcher.
'Let's go and take a look,' said Ford.

They returned to the tractor and Ford carefully dug round the object buried in the soil. After a little while he and Butcher managed to lift it out of the hole. It was a huge plate covered all over with a green crust. Ford was tremen-
20   dously excited, but he tried to hide his excitement. Meanwhile Butcher was still kneeling beside the hole. 'There's something else here,' he said and up came another plate. Eventually they found thirty-four separate pieces.

By now it had begun to snow and the two men were dreadfully cold. Butcher, who was totally unaware of the value of their find, was keen to get home to
25   a warm fire and a nice hot cup of tea; but Ford was pretty certain that they had just dug up a hoard of Roman silver. If it was Roman silver it would be worth a fortune and he was wondering desperately how he could keep it all for himself.

There was a problem and he knew it. In England there is a law which states
30   that any object made of gold or silver that is found buried automatically becomes the property of the state. Provided that the find is reported to the

police immediately the finder will receive from the government the full value of the 'treasure'.

Since Butcher had actually found the silver, it was he who would get the
35 reward if the find were reported. Because of this Ford decided to keep silent about the discovery and hoped that Butcher would do the same. The amazing thing is that Butcher seems to have thought little more of the matter until an archaeologist visiting Ford some four years later noticed two Roman spoons and persuaded him to go to the police. Then of course the police
40 came to see Butcher and both men were ordered to appear at a special court hearing.

Eventually both Butcher and Ford received a token payment of £1,000 each and the silver went to the British Museum where it can be seen today. It is known as 'The Mildenhall Treasure'.

B Multiple choice questions

Choose the best answer.

1 Gordon Butcher was ploughing a field when

a a metal object stopped the tractor.
b the plough hit something made of silver.
c he saw a green metal plate in the soil.
d the tractor hit an object buried in the earth.

2 a Butcher was a highly educated man.
b Butcher was used to finding Roman objects.
c Butcher was employed by Ford.
d Butcher was a friend of Ford's.

3 Ford was more excited about the find than Butcher because

a he was better educated than Butcher.
b he was hoping to make a profit out of the discovery.
c he was more interested in Roman items than Butcher.
d he was planning to report the find to the authorities and receive the reward.

4 If you found

a an old steel sword in England, it would automatically belong to the state.
b some silver coins, you could keep them.
c a collection of prehistoric iron tools and reported the find, the state would reward you.
d an old gold bracelet and reported the find, you would receive some money from the state.

5 a Butcher was extremely lucky to receive £1,000.
b Ford was unlucky to receive a reward of only £1,000.
c An archaeologist told the police about the silver.
d Ford knowingly broke the law.

C Word study

Look at the following from the text:
The **amazing** thing is that Butcher seems to have thought little more of the matter . . . (ll. 36–37)

Amazing things happen, and people, too, can be amazing. Think of Nicky Lauda, Winston Churchill or Napoleon Bonaparte.

People can also be:

boastful praising oneself too much
courageous very brave
hungry in need of food
idle lazy
knowledgeable knowing a lot
nasty unpleasant
patient prepared to wait calmly for something
polite having good manners and behaving considerately towards other people

stupid foolish, not intelligent
thirsty in need of something to drink
wasteful using more than is necessary
wicked very bad, immoral
wise having learnt from experience to make good judgements

Study the table below, then work with a partner and fill in the missing items. Use your dictionary where necessary.

Noun	Adjective	Adverb
amazement	amazing	amazingly
	boastful	
	courageous	
	hungry	
	idle	
	knowledgeable	
	nasty	
	patient	
	polite	
	stupid	
	thirsty	
	wasteful	
	wicked	
	wise	

D Word study

Fill the gaps in the following sentences with suitable words from the table in section C.

Example Blériot was the first man to fly across the Channel. It seemed an .... feat at the time.

Answer amazing

1 'I'm awfully sorry,' said Jenkins, 'but my .... of Spanish is limited.'

2 He's certainly not a fool, but he'll never pass the exam. He's too ....

3 It was hot and the horses stopped at the pool and drank ....

4 He was very .... to Samantha. He said her new hairstyle didn't suit her at all.

5 She began to get very severe headaches, so she .... went to see her doctor.

6 Housing those old people on the top floor of that block of flats was an act of great ....

7 It would be a complete .... of time to try to persuade her to change her mind.

8 John's been telling everyone how well he played. He's been behaving in a very .... manner.

9 The waiter bowed .... and showed Henderson and his wife to a table near the window.

10 The brave young policeman disarmed the gunman. It was a very .... action.

E Word study

Notice the phrase:
Because of this, Ford decided . . . (l. 35)

Study these similar phrases, used in context:

According to the map, we should be almost there.
I'm sure you'll have nothing to complain about **as regards** the climate.

You won't have to pay for anything $\left\{ \begin{array}{l} \textbf{except for} \\ \textbf{apart from} \end{array} \right\}$ your drinks.

He never enjoyed being **away from** his family.
Ahead of him, outlined against the sky, he could see the great castle.
We reached the mountain restaurant **by means of** the ski lift.
Instead of the steak I'm going to have fish.
On reaching the top of the cliffs we found that it was impossible to see

the lighthouse $\left\{ \begin{array}{l} \textbf{due to} \\ \textbf{on account of} \\ \textbf{owing to} \\ \textbf{because of} \end{array} \right\}$ the fog.

The children enjoyed themselves **in spite of** the rain.
On behalf of myself, Miss Plunkett and all the staff, I should like to congratulate you on your promotion.

$\left. \begin{array}{l} \textbf{As well as} \\ \textbf{Apart from} \\ \textbf{In addition to} \end{array} \right\}$ being fined, he was given a severe warning as to his future conduct.

Now read the following account of an attempt at a new athletics record. Then fill the gaps with suitable phrases from the examples above.

(1) .... one observer who knows Geoffrey well, the attempt at the record was almost abandoned in the morning. The weather forecast was not good and (2) .... this, Chris seemed to be developing a cold. (3) .... these early setbacks, however, the three athletes involved agreed that it was a case of now or never. (4) .... the approaching exams, revision for which would take a lot of time, there was the question of Phil's visit to Ottawa. He would be (5) .... Durham for at least a fortnight. So, (6) .... waiting to see how the weather turned out, it was decided to go ahead with the attempt that evening, come what may. About 6 o'clock there was a shower of rain and (7) .... this, it was decided to postpone the attempt for an hour. At exactly 7.30 the three runners stripped off their track suits and settled down at the start, with four laps of the damp, black cinder track (8) .... them. At approximately 7.35 Geoffrey crossed the finishing line, and the record was his. Less than five years later, at Oxford, Roger Bannister ran the first sub-four-minute mile.

F Focus on grammar: second conditional

Study these sentences from the text in section A:

If it was Roman silver, it would be worth a fortune . . . (ll. 26–27)
. . . he . . . would get the reward if the find were reported. (ll. 34–35)

In this type of conditional sentence, the pattern is:

if+past simple, **would**+infinitive without **to**

Since the past tense is actually subjunctive, when the verb in the *if* clause is *to be*
were is often used instead of **was**.
We use the second conditional when talking about suppositions and events that
might possibly occur. Here are some more examples:

As it is so cold, the men wear gloves. If they **didn't wear** gloves, they **would get**
frostbite.
If there **were** no policemen, there **would be** a lot more crime.
If she **had** enough money, she **would learn** to fly. (But she hasn't got enough
money.)

When the second conditional is used, there is often an implication that the matter
being discussed is unlikely to occur.

G Grammar practice

Work in pairs. Answer the following questions as honestly as possible:

1   If you won a holiday competition and could go anywhere, where would you choose
    to go?

2   If you could have dinner at a luxury hotel with any famous person you wished, who
    would you have dinner with? What do you think you would talk about?

3   If you were so talented that you could take up any career you wanted, what career
    would you decide on? How do you think you would spend your working hours?

4   If it was your birthday next week and you could have any three-course meal you
    wanted, what would you choose? What would you have to drink with your meal?

5   If you were a famous writer or artist and could live and work anywhere in the
    world, where would you go? How would you spend your weekends?

H Focus on grammar: conditionals

The first and second conditionals can be expressed in other ways:

a **Supposing** John loses his job, how will he pay his rent?
Supposing John were to become ill, he might lose his job.

In the examples above, **supposing** is used as an alternative to **if**. In the second example, **would** is replaced by **might**, indicating a *possible* result of John's becoming ill. **Could** is another alternative.

b You can borrow the book **provided that** you promise to give it back.

Here **if** is replaced by the phrase **provided that**, which is nearly always used with the **first conditional**.

c Sometimes the **second conditional** is expressed by using **were** at the beginning of the sentence. This construction is more likely to be used in written than spoken English.

Were I to lend you the money, when would you be in a position to pay me back?
Were he aware of how worried she is, I am sure he would write.

I Grammar practice

Write the second sentences in 1–10 so that they mean the same as the first ones:

Examples How long would the journey take if they came by coach?
Supposing . . .
Supposing they came by coach, how long would the journey take?

I'll come to the wedding if I don't have to make a speech.
Provided that . . .
Provided that I don't have to make a speech, I'll come to the wedding.

If you listened to her yourself, I think you might feel differently.
Were . . .
Were you to listen to her yourself, I think you might feel differently.

1 I will sing if you promise to play the guitar.
Provided that . . .

2 What would we do if we missed the last train?
Supposing . . .

3 I would let you borrow the car if it were mine.
Were . . .

4 I'll be happy to give you a lift if you are at my house by two o'clock.
Provided that . . .

5 How would you feel about it if Peter got the job?
Supposing . . .

6 John will get you a copy of the book if it is still available.
Provided that . . .

7   I would support them if they were prepared to work really hard at the project.
Were . . .

8   Do you really want to go to university if you pass all your examinations?
Supposing . . .

9   I think you might enjoy the film very much if you saw it.
Were . . .

10   People might talk to one another more if there were no television.
Supposing . . .

J Grammar practice

How well do you know the other members of your class?

Choose a partner, not necessarily someone sitting near you. Study the following situations and decide how your partner would react in each situation.

Your partner must also decide how you would react.

When you have both finished, compare your answers.

1   Your partner is kept waiting for thirty-five minutes outside a restaurant. Would he/she

a   get very annoyed and grumble when his/her date finally arrived?
b   eventually go and sit down inside the restaurant and study the menu?
c   wait patiently outside the restaurant until his/her date arrived and remain cheerful?

2   Your partner wins an expensive box of chocolates in a raffle at a party. Would he/she

a   open the box at once and offer chocolates to the other guests?
b   take the box home and offer the chocolates to his/her family and friends?
c   take the box home and eat all the chocolates himself/herself?

3   One summer evening, at a party, your partner is pushed, fully dressed, into a swimming pool. Would he/she

a   become absolutely furious and insist on going home?
b   get mad for a little while, but soon realize it was only a joke?
c   laugh as loudly as everyone else?

4   Your partner is woken in the middle of the night by the sound of a woman screaming in the house next door. Would he/she

a   go next door at once and ring the bell?
b   telephone the police and report the screams?
c   cover his/her head with the bedclothes and go back to sleep?

5   Three times in the last week your partner has suffered a sharp pain in his/her chest. It didn't last long, but it was very painful. Would he/she

a   make an appointment to see the doctor?
b   speak to a friend about it?
c   say nothing and hope it would not happen again?

K *Focus on grammar:* verb+infinitive verb+gerund

Look at these sentences from the reading text:

He immediately **stopped** . . . **to see** what the object was. (ll. 3–4)
. . . he and Butcher **managed to lift** it out of the hole. (l. 18)
. . . but he **tried to hide** his excitement. (l. 20)
Ford **decided to keep** silent about the discovery . . . (ll. 35–36)
. . . an archaeologist . . . **persuaded him to go** to the police. (ll. 38–39)
. . . Butcher **seems to have thought** little more of the matter . . . (l. 37) (perfect infinitive)

In Unit 5 we practised using certain verbs followed by a gerund. The verbs **love**, **hate**, **prefer** and **remember** can be used in this way when we are talking about activities or past actions, but they are usually followed by an infinitive in future or conditional situations.

Examples   She **prefers dancing** to studying. (activity)
She **would love to go** to the party. (conditional situation)
I **hated telling** her the news. (past action)
You must **remember to telephone** her. (future action)

The verb **try** is followed by an infinitive when it means **attempt** and by a gerund when it means **experiment**.

Examples   They **tried to start** the engine, but without success.
Have you **tried soaking** the seeds in water before you plant them?

The verb **stop** is followed by an infinitive when we can use **in order to** after it and a gerund when it expresses the idea of something coming to an end or finishing.

Examples   He **stopped (in order) to remove** the paper from the chocolate.
After his illness he **stopped performing** in public.

L *Grammar practice*

Look at what these people said and then answer the questions on page 90:

Frances said: 'I enjoy cooking very much indeed.'
John said: 'Enid, you won't forget to post the letter, will you?'
Alice said: 'I couldn't start the car, so I had to walk.'
Grandfather said: 'One day, when I was a boy, we visited the lighthouse.'
Mrs Scott said: 'I don't go to that restaurant any more. I had a terrible argument there with one of the waiters.'
Jerry said: 'If you don't mind, I'd rather stay at home this evening.'
Tony said: 'Hold on a moment. I want to make a telephone call.'
Robert said: 'I certainly wouldn't like to be famous.'
One of the scientists said: 'We've sprayed the crops with pesticide from an aeroplane, but even that wasn't successful.'

Example   Who remembers doing what?
Grandfather remembers visiting the lighthouse.

1   Who must remember to do what?

2   Who would hate what?

3   Who has stopped doing what? Why?

4   Who loves doing what?

5   Who tried to do what?

6   Who would prefer to do what?

7   Who tried doing what?

8   Who stopped to do what?

M *Listening comprehension*

Listen to this radio discussion, then answer the questions.

1   What does Richard Anthony do?

2   How big is the synthesizer?

3   What colour are the keys?

4   Can the synthesizer be played through speakers?

5   Can the synthesizer produce stereo sound?

6   Where was the synthesizer made?

7   Write the names of two rhythms the synthesizer will produce.

8   Write the names of two instruments the synthesizer can imitate.

9   How much does it cost?

10   How could you purchase one of these synthesizers if you couldn't pay cash?

N *Writing activity*

Write 120–180 words on 'Music in my life'.

Write three paragraphs. In the first, write about your favourite kind(s) of music. In the second write about any types of music you are not keen on and explain why. Use the third paragraph to finish off with one or two general remarks about the importance of music in your life.

◼ O *Communicative practice:* complaints

Excuse me, ... Do you think (you) could ....?	Yes, of course, (sir/madam). Certainly, (sir/madam).
Excuse me, ... Would you mind —ing ....?	No, of course not.
Look, I'm sorry to have to complain, but	Oh, I *am* sorry. I'll ....

Model conversations

1 a Excuse me, this coffee's cold. Do you think I could have another cup?

b Yes, of course, sir. *or* Certainly, sir.

Work in pairs. Use the situations in the box to make similar conversations.

In a restaurant:

there's no salt
you have a dirty knife
the steak is tough
there's only one bread roll
there's a crack in your glass

2 a Excuse me, I bought this shirt for my brother, but it has a mark on the collar. Would you mind changing it?

b No, of course not.

Continue working in pairs. Use the situations in the box to make similar conversations.

The pullover you bought yesterday had the wrong size marked on the packet.

You took some letters to be copied. When you got home, you found that the quality of the copies was very bad.

The radio you bought last week isn't working properly.

You bought 2lb of pears and you found that some of them were badly damaged.

The watch you had cleaned keeps stopping.

3 a   Look, I'm sorry to have to complain, but your dog frightened the life out of my wife this morning.

  b   Oh, I *am* sorry. I'll make sure he doesn't get through to the front again.

Continue working in pairs. Use the situations in the box to make similar conversations. In each case **b** *should apologize and offer to take some action as a result of the complaint.*

> Your next-door neighbour is in his garden with his radio, which is on terribly loud.
>
> Someone keeps parking his car in front of your gate so that you can't get your car out.
>
> The people in the flat next door had a party last night. It was very noisy and went on very late.
>
> Your telephone was repaired last week. It's gone wrong again.
>
> It's eleven o'clock at night and the man in the flat below is making a terrible noise hammering nails into wood.

•• P Dialogue

Listen to the dialogue twice, without looking at it, then answer the following questions:

1   Why was £590 'a ridiculous figure'?

2   What is Ted's telephone number? How exactly did Ted say it?

3   How did the computer arrive at a figure of £531?

4   What does Ted want the telephone company to send him? Why do you think he wants this?

5   Apart from sending him this, what does the woman promise to do?

Voice   Ted is telephoning the accounts department of British Telecom about his telephone bill.

  Ted   Hello, is that the accounts department?

Woman   Yes, accounts department here.

  Ted   Look, I'm sorry to have to complain, but there's a problem with my account.

Woman   Yes?

  Ted   You sent me a bill for £590.

Woman	Yes . . .
Ted	Well, that was a ridiculous figure.
Woman	I see. What is your name, sir?
Ted	Carter. E. S. Carter, 2, Thorbell Drive, Sydenham.
Woman	What's your telephone number, sir?
Ted	372 4255.
Woman	Hold on a moment, please . . . Well, according to our records, you owe £531, sir.
Ted	Yes, but that's just the point. You sent me a bill for £590. I rang you up about it and was told it was a computer error. It should have been £59. So I sent you a cheque for £59 and I've just had another bill for £531.
Woman	I see. I'm very sorry, sir. Leave it with me and I'll sort it out.
Ted	Well, I hope you will. Do you want me to return this bill?
Woman	No, that won't be necessary, sir.
Ted	Would you mind sending me a receipt for the £59?
Woman	No, we'll do that, sir.
Ted	All right. Thank you.
Woman	Thank you, sir. Bye.
Ted	Goodbye.

Q *Writing activity*

A letter of complaint to: Sherwood's Ltd, 8, Forest Road, Nottingham.

Through Sherwood's mail order catalogue, you ordered a pair of 7×50 binoculars. The price was £40, of which you have paid a deposit of £10.

When the binoculars arrived, you had two reasons to be dissatisfied:

a The parcel contained a pair of 10×50 binoculars, which are not suitable.

b The binoculars had been damaged in the post. In your opinion they were not very well packed.

You decide to return the binoculars.

Write a suitable letter to enclose in the parcel. You will need 100–140 words.

Unit 8   Gifts of Passage

A Reading comprehension

Study the following words and phrases before you read the text.

an educational circuit a journey
  of discovery and learning
in retrospect looking back
an indelible engagement with India
  a very strong identification with India
allegiance loyalty

deploring regretting and
  disapproving of
that have plagued me that have
  troubled me
a paycheck American spelling for
  'a pay cheque'
quirk strange way of behaving

Gifts of Passage

My mother very sensibly decided that my sister and I should make an educational circuit of this new-old land which was both our home and so foreign.
Most of that voyage of exploration, which took us all over India with relatives,
friends, strangers, and involved us in innumerable situations and lives, I
5   recorded some years ago in a book called *Home to India*. In retrospect,
although I was at no regular school, they seem to me the two most important
years of my education. Even though they ended in my going to college in
America, they left me with an indelible engagement with India – an engagement that even now, when I am married to an American, have a child who
10   divides his allegiance between America and India, have lived so many more
years outside my own country, never entirely leaves me and never allows me
to escape from an almost automatic concern with India. I make a very poor
expatriate.

My four years in America were spent mostly at Wellesley College, with
15   vacation intervals of working for the Office of War Information. It was a
strange time for me – half in love with America, with its driving energy, its
earnestness, its kindness, and its extraordinary beauty, half deploring its
ignorance of conditions in the rest of the world, its smug self-righteousness,
and its assumption of privilege. Anyway, out of the whole experience emerged
20   two things that have plagued me all my life. I realized that I wanted to be a
writer (my first book was written while I was at Wellesley) and I had somehow
learned to work – not simply to work but to want to work. The phrase 'career
girl' was already unfashionable by then, but by the time I returned, once
again, to India it was clear that a 'career girl' was what I was going to be.
25   America gave me not only the freedom but the compulsion to feel this way,
and also a kind of sadness that a whole era of my early life was irretrievably
lost. The world – and I with it – had moved too fast.

As soon as I got back to Bombay, the year the war ended, I set about looking
for a job. My family didn't mind my working, but they were worried about
30   the idea of my earning money. It wasn't considered entirely respectable for
a girl whose family could afford to support her until she got married to be
actually picking up a paycheck. By then I felt rather militant about the whole

situation and insisted with many cheeky arguments that work should be paid for. It says a lot for the broad-mindedness of my parents that they
35 indulged me in this unconventional quirk and allowed me to take a job on a magazine in Bombay.

From *Gifts of Passage* by Santha Rama Rau

B Multiple choice questions

Choose the best answer.

1 The writer

a is half Indian and half American.
b spent two years travelling round India with her mother.
c feels she learnt more travelling than she did at Wellesley College.
d was at one time engaged to an Indian.

2 During the four years that the writer was in the U.S.A., she

a worked during the holidays.
b did research at the Office of War Information.
c married an American.
d sometimes felt very strange.

3 The writer's first book

a was recorded for radio.
b was called *Home to India*.
c was written in America.
d was published in India.

4 The writer feels sad because

a she decided to become a career girl.
b she knows she disappointed her parents.
c she feels she has wasted a great deal of time.
d she was changed by her American experience.

5 Respectable girls

a didn't work till they were married.
b didn't take a paid job before they were married.
c didn't collect their pay cheques themselves.
d didn't work on magazines.

C Word study

Choose the words or phrases which best complete the following sentences. Indicate where there is more than one acceptable answer. Explain why the remaining words or phrases are unsuitable.

1 Stop complaining. George has made a very .... suggestion. We'll take a taxi.

   a sensational **b** reasonable **c** practical **d** sensible **e** sensitive

2 Jones wasn't .... in the robbery at any stage.

   a indicated **b** installed **c** instituted **d** invested **e** involved

3 A police spokesman last night expressed .... for the safety of the missing child.

   a fright **b** fear **c** worry **d** anxiety **e** concern

4 Tom's not here, I'm afraid. He went .... last week.

   a on holiday **b** in holiday **c** on vacation **d** in vacation **e** on leave

5 Be honest. Are you going to .... my proposal, or not?

   a back **b** object **c** oppose **d** support **e** agree

6 We argued for a long time, but .... he agreed to give me a job.

   a in the end **b** at the end **c** finally **d** eventually **e** at last

7 I'm not prepared to .... you £5,000 for the new car.

   a afford **b** spend **c** pay **d** lend **e** borrow

8 In my opinion the manager spoke very .... to his employees.

   a rudely **b** honest **c** cheekily **d** impolite **e** unfair

D Word study

Note these phrasal verbs used in the text in section A:

As soon as I **got back** to Bombay, . . . I **set about** looking for a job. (ll. 28–29)

Here are some more useful phrasal verbs, all of which we use when talking about the things people do.
Match them with the definitions below:

back out (of)	**check out**	**hang on**
break down	**count on**	**let down**
bring round	**drop off**	**pass away**
catch on	**get over**	**pass out**
check in	**give up**	**take after**

1 understand:

2 register (at reception in a hotel or for a flight at an airport):

3 go to sleep:

4 faint (lose consciousness):

5 die:

6 rely on:

7 lose control of one's emotions and cry:

8 officially give up one's room at a hotel:

9 assist (someone) to regain consciousness:

10 recover from (illness or sorrow):

11 wait (for a short time):

12 resemble (one's father, mother, grandfather, etc.):

13 disappoint (someone) by failing to keep a promise:

14 surrender:

15 withdraw from an agreement (often when someone is relying on your support):

E Word study

Now complete the following sentences by using a suitable phrasal verb from the list in section D:

1   Stephen was so tired that he .... in the middle of the film.

2   By the time George arrived at the hotel, he found that his wife had already ....

3   Since Simon wasn't terribly intelligent, it took him a little while to ....

4   Unfortunately the President .... during the night. The funeral will take place on Friday.

5   Roy's father .... and wept when he heard the news that his son was safe.

6   .... a moment. I've forgotten my tennis racket.

7   The old man never really .... the death of his wife.

8   I think young Frank .... his mother. He has her eyes.

9   Come on. We're not going to .... now. It's only another fifty feet or so to the top.

10 I hope we can .... your support during the election.

11 Look, you promised to speak at the meeting, and you're not going to .... now.

12 In cowboy films they always seem to .... the man who loses the fight by throwing a bucket of water over him.

F Focus on grammar: clauses of concession

Look at these two sentences from the text. Notice particularly the words in **bold** type:

. . . **although I was at no regular school**, they seem to me the two most important years of my education. (ll. 6–7)

Even though they ended in my going to college in America, they left me with an indelible engagement with India. (ll. 7–8)

We call constructions like this, clauses of concession. Look at some more examples:

Although the women worked the same hours as the men, they earned 30 per cent less.
Though it rained a lot, we had quite a pleasant holiday.
However hard you train, you will never make a top-class athlete.

Note that when we use 'however' in clauses of concession, it must be followed by an *adjective* or an *adverb*.

Also note that in written English 'however'+adjective/adverb is often followed by 'may' or 'might'.

Examples   **However angry he may be** about it now, he will eventually realize that we are doing it for his own good.
He's a salesman and he has to go abroad occasionally, **however much his wife might miss him**.

I'm going to marry Peter, **even if you don't approve**.

In written English 'even if' is sometimes followed by 'should' or an emphatically stressed verb.

Examples   **Even if George should be there**, he won't recognize you with that beard.
He ought not to talk to people so rudely, **even if he *is* a famous actor.**
I'm not going to work on Saturday, **even if they do offer me overtime**.

G *Grammar practice*

Finish each of the incomplete sentences in such a way that it means exactly the same as the sentence before it.

Example   It might rain, but we shall still go for a picnic.
Even if . . .
Even if it rains, we shall still go for a picnic.

1   There weren't many people at the party. However, everybody had a good time.
Although . . .

2   It's rather late, but I think I'll ring him up.
Though . . .

3   You wouldn't catch the train, even if you drove very fast.
However . . .

4   However nice the new flat is, they'll miss their old home.
Even if . . .

5   He worked very hard. However, he didn't pass the examination.
Although . . .

6   She sang very well, but she didn't win the competition.
Even though . . .

7   He must have the operation, even if he is nervous about it.
However . . .

8   There were several strong candidates for the job, but George got it.
George got . . .

9   Getting lost is no problem, because you can always ask someone the way.
Even if you . . .

10 His qualifications might be very good, but he won't get a job there.
However . . .

H Focus on Grammar: reported speech 2

In unit 3 we practised using reported speech for statements and questions in the present simple, past simple and present perfect.

Study the chart below, which shows the changes that occur when other structures are used:

Direct Speech	Reported speech
Fred: '**I'm seeing** George tomorrow.'	Fred *told* me he **was seeing** George today.
George: '**I'm going to sell** the car.'	George *said* he **was going to sell** the car.
Barbara: 'Harry, **I'll never forget** you.'	Barbara *promised* Harry she **would never forget** him.
Sheila: '**I've been looking** at the photographs.'	Sheila *announced* (that) she **had been looking** at the photographs.
Mick: '**I was working** on the roof.'	Mick *insisted* (that) he **had been working** on the roof.
Frank: 'Helen, **give** Tony the money.'	Frank *told* Helen **to give** Tony the money.
Helen: 'Please **don't tell** anyone, Tom.'	Helen *asked* Tom **not to tell** anyone.

I Grammar practice

Chicago. 1925. A number of famous gangsters are meeting in a secret location, behind a Chinese restaurant. The Chairman is Fats Galento, and they are discussing their business activities.

Fats O.K. Gloria. Listen to what everyone says. Write it down and then type out a report for me. I want it on my desk by ten o'clock tomorrow morning. O.K. gentlemen, I want to know what you've been doing and what you're planning to do during the next three months. Fingers, you start.

Fingers We've been concentrating on the dog tracks. I now control all four dog tracks in the city.

Fats Luigi . . .

Luigi My gang controls the night spots on the west side of town, but we've been having problems with the Palm Tree Restaurant on Thirty-fourth Street. Everybody keep away from there on Saturday night. If the protection money isn't paid by then, there's going to be a mysterious explosion.

Fats	Big Schultz?
Big Schultz	We've been robbing banks. We've robbed most of the banks in Chicago, but we won't be robbing any more for a while. We have in mind a very profitable kidnapping. Unfortunately I am unable to give any further details at this time.
Fats	We understand, Big Schultz. Thank you gentlemen for being so frank. Does anybody want to ask any questions? O.K. I declare the meeting closed.

You are Gloria. Write the report, as requested by Fats. Use a new paragraph for each speaker, beginning like this:
Fats wanted to know what everyone had been doing and what they . . .

J Listening comprehension

Listen to the radio panel discussion on the subject of smoking in public, then answer the following questions. You will hear the discussion twice.

1 Where does the girl who asks the question come from?

2 Would you say Ken is **a** for **b** against **c** indifferent to   smoking in public?

3 What particular phrase does Ken use that makes his opinion clear?

4 Would you say Barbara is **a** for **b** against **c** indifferent to   smoking in public?

5 In her first contribution to the discussion Barbara uses three heavily stressed words which make her attitude very clear. Write them down:
a .... **b** .... **c** ....

6 Would you describe Barbara's remarks to the young man who asked if he might smoke as **a** unfair **b** aggressive **c** sarcastic?

7 What about Robert? What is his attitude to smoking?

8 Complete this sentence: Robert has smoked for at least . . .

9 How old was Robert's grandfather when he died?

10 Robert introduces his grandfather into the discusson for which of the following reasons:
a as an argument in favour of smoking cigarettes?
b as a warning of the dangers of smoking?
c to show that smoking isn't necessarily bad for you?

Discussion

When people talk seriously about a subject like smoking, they often reveal quite a lot about their own characters. Think about Ken, Barbara and Robert. What did they reveal about themselves during their discussion?

K Writing activity

Talk about smoking.
The dangers of smoking receive a lot of publicity these days, don't they?
What are the dangers of smoking?
Have they been exaggerated?
Do you smoke?
Do your friends or family smoke?
How much do they smoke?

In old movies the hero nearly always smoked, didn't he?
Often the heroine did too. Why do you think this was?
What was the image the film-makers were trying to create?
What sort of person smoked   **a** cigars?   **b** a pipe?   **c** cigarettes?

Write three paragraphs on 'Society's changing attitude to smoking'.

In your first paragraph describe what people's attitude to smoking used to be thirty or forty years ago. In your second paragraph write about how people regard smoking now and explain why people's attitudes have changed. Start your final paragraph by saying whether you yourself smoke or not and go on to explain how you personally feel about smoking.

Write between 120 and 180 words.

L Communicative practice: advice

Do you think I should . . .?	If I were you, I'd . . .
I don't know whether to . . .	If you take my advice, you'll . . .
Would you advise me to . . .?	I think you ought to . . .

Model conversations

1 a Do you think I should buy the green curtains or the blue ones?

b If I were you, I'd buy the green ones. They'll match the chair covers.

Work in pairs. Use the phrases in the box to make similar conversations. Try and find a reason for the advice you choose to give.

buy Sarah the red gloves or the brown gloves
go to the party or stay at home
leave my hair as it is or have it cut short
open the red wine or the white wine
get a video recorder or a home computer

2 a I've got a pain in my chest. I don't know whether to go to the doctor or not.

b If you take my advice, you'll go and see the doctor at once.

Continue working in pairs. Use the phrases in the box to make similar conversations. This time you must decide exactly what advice to give.

I've got toothache.

My television isn't working properly.

There's a smell of gas in my kitchen.

I'm having problems starting my car.

My eyes have been hurting.

---

3 a Would you advise me to keep the money in my bank account?

b I think you ought to see the manager and find out as much as you can about interest rates.

Continue working in pairs. Use the phrases in the box to make similar conversations. In this type of situation the person asking for advice is really asking for confirmation that he/she has made a sensible decision. Try and think of circumstances to suit each situation.

---

see a lawyer

speak to my boss about it

contact the insurance company

mention it to my doctor

stop taking the medicine

•• *M* *Dialogue*

Listen to the whole of the dialogue twice, without looking at the script, then answer the following questions:

1 Who asked to see whom?

2 Who is Angela?

3 Did Andy get the new job?

4 What went wrong?

5 Why did Andy think Norman might be in a position to give him some useful advice?

6 Norman advised Andy to go and talk to three men. Who were they?

7 Which sum of money will Andy almost certainly lose? Why will he lose this?

8 Why do you think Andy hasn't told Angela the news?

Work in pairs. Listen to the first part of the dialogue again, looking at the script. Then take the parts of Andy and Norman and practise reading it.
Listen to the second and third parts of the dialogue in turn and practise reading these.

Part 1

Andy has had some bad luck and has made an appointment to see an old friend called Norman.

Norman   Hello Andy, you wanted to see me.

Andy   Yes, it's awfully good of you to give up your time . . .

Norman   Not at all. I was very happy to hear from you. We haven't met since last Christmas. How's Angela?

Andy   Oh, fine, fine.

Norman   You said on the telephone that you had a bit of a problem.

Andy   Yes . . . um . . . I'd like your advice. Do you remember at Christmas I told you I was planning to change my job?

Norman   Yes, you'd been for an interview, if I remember . . .

Andy   That's right. With Hodson and Palmer. Well, I got the job; very nice, £2,000 a year increase in salary. Angela gave up working. We moved to Esher. But suddenly everything's turned sour.

Norman   The job didn't work out?

Andy   Hodson and Palmer are being taken over by an American firm and I'm being made redundant. I've just bought a new car, I've put down a deposit on a flat. I thought you, being an accountant . . . you might have some ideas . . .

Part 2

Norman Mmm . . . Have you got any money in the bank?

Andy No, I've got an overdraft.

Norman A big overdraft?

Andy About £300.

Norman Have you talked to your bank manager?

Andy No, I haven't talked to anybody yet. I only got the news yesterday.

Norman Well, I'd advise you to go and have a chat with your bank manager as soon as possible. Be absolutely honest with him. Don't forget he's used to dealing with situations like this.

Andy Do you reckon I'll lose the deposit I paid on the flat?

Norman Not necessarily. If I were you, I'd go and see the house agent. Explain the position and say you want to withdraw from the contract.

Part 3

Andy What about the car?

Norman Yes, you've got a problem there. You didn't pay cash, I suppose?

Andy No, I put down £1,000 deposit, with the balance to be paid over two years.

Norman The problem is that it's no longer a new car. But again I think you ought to go back to the chap you bought it from and explain the position. He'll probably be able to sell it for a decent price, in which case you won't be too much out of pocket.

Andy But I won't get my deposit back?

Norman Oh, I'm afraid that's very unlikely . . . Is there any chance of Angela getting her old job back?

Andy I don't know. I haven't even told her yet.

Norman Well, if you take my advice, you'll go straight home and tell Angela about it, see the bank manager and those other chaps tomorrow, then stop worrying about money and concentrate on finding another job.

Andy Yes . . . yes, I'm sure you're right. Thanks Norman. Thanks very much.

N Writing activity

In Units 5 and 7 you studied verbs which are followed by a gerund or an infinitive. This exercise will give you more practice in using some of these verbs.

Below is some information about ten lonely people who have asked an agency to try and find them a suitable marriage partner.

Imagine you are employed by the agency. Study the report on Angela and Bill, then the details given about each person. Choose three more couples and write similar reports (approximately 50 words on each couple), explaining why the people involved should be introduced to one another.

Example **Angela and Bill**

Angela can't bear people smoking near her. She avoids going to crowded places and likes the idea of living in the country. **Bill** also doesn't like to see people smoking and enjoys going for long walks. He is 25 and she is 24. They might make a suitable couple.

 Angela 24, can't bear people smoking near her. She avoids going to crowded places. She fancies living in the country.

 Kevin 29, enjoys eating tasty food. He doesn't mind looking after his sister's children. He prefers going out to watching TV.

 Arthur 25, delays making decisions as long as possible. He hates getting up in the morning. He doesn't mind doing housework.

 Wendy 25, sometimes imagines meeting a very rich man. She enjoys going to romantic films with her mother. She likes living on her own.

 Bill 25, loves watching sport on TV. He enjoys going for long walks. He dislikes seeing people smoking.

 Roger 31, enjoys travelling. He can't stand being alone. He admits to losing his temper rather easily.

 Valerie 25, loves cooking. She enjoys going to the cinema. She is looking forward to having children of her own one day.

 Brenda 29, stopped smoking recently. She can't help thinking about food. She enjoys being with a lot of friends.

 Helen 30, hates wasting time. she admits to being rather bossy. She doesn't fancy being a mother.

 Victor 32, admits to being bad-tempered in the morning. He can't stand dogs. He dislikes having children around.

Unit 9   *Hypnotism*

A *Reading comprehension*

Study the following words and phrases before you read the text.

hypnotism the practice of putting a person into a dream-like state
contemporaries people who lived at the same time as he did
very odd strange, almost crazy
asthma a disease which makes breathing difficult
hypnosis a dream-like state

it transpired it was discovered, it became known
inducing causing
a verbal trigger a word or phrase that acts as a signal for some action
limp weak, lacking in strength
insomnia inability to sleep
links connections

Hypnotism

Those who work in the entertainment profession are well aware of the importance of a name. If the inventor of the word hypnotism had had a serious, German-sounding name like Jung, or Freud, or Einstein, people might have treated his ideas with more respect. As it was, Dr James Braid was regarded
5 by many of his contemporaries as very odd, and even today the value of his work tends to be underestimated.

Let us imagine that you were suffering from asthma. If you went to see your doctor he would probably prescribe pills or an inhalant, but if you asked him if he thought hypnosis might help, it is most unlikely that he would agree.
10 Some doctors might even get quite annoyed at your suggesting such a thing. Yet a report published by a sub-committee of the British Medical Association in 1955 clearly stated that hypnotism had a part to play in medicine.

It is possible to put most people into a hypnotic state, but contrary to popular belief, they will not normally carry out an action suggested by the hypnotist
15 if there is some particular reason for their not agreeing to it. For instance, a lady under hypnosis was asked to play an imaginary piano. Although she had already obeyed various instructions, she would not play the piano. It transpired that as a child she had been forced to take piano lessons, which she hated.

20 There are various ways of inducing a hypnotic state in people. They may be asked to gaze at a lighted candle, to watch a swinging pendulum, to stare into the eyes of the hypnotist, or to breathe deeply. Frequently the hypnotist will use a verbal trigger . . . 'When I say *relax* I want you to let all the tension go out of your body, your body is going to feel completely limp . . . you're
25 going to be filled with a pleasant heaviness . . . ready . . . *relax* . . .'

Hypnotism is sometimes used to treat patients suffering from nervous tension or insomnia, and it can also be of help to those who find difficulty in giving up smoking. Nevertheless, until recently, little interest has been shown in the subject by the medical profession as a whole. However, with
30 the growing awareness of the close links between mental stress and actual physical illness, it is likely that this form of treatment may be more widely used by doctors in the future.

B *Multiple choice questions*

Choose the best answer.

1 a James Braid invented hypnotism.
  b James Braid was a little mad.
  c James Braid was the first person to use the word 'hypnotism'.
  d James Braid was an entertainer.

2 The report published in 1955 suggested

  a that doctors should learn more about hypnotism.
  b that hypnotism might be a useful form of treatment.
  c that doctors should have nothing to do with hypnotism.
  d that hypnotism might help patients more than pills.

3 The woman refused to play the imaginary piano because

  a she hadn't enjoyed learning to play the piano.
  b she had been taught very badly.
  c she was tired of carrying out the hypnotist's instructions.
  d she very much disliked the sound of the piano.

4 People being hypnotized

  a are asked to look carefully at a lighted candle.
  b are occasionally told to watch an object swinging from side to side.
  c are usually instructed to look into the eyes of the hypnotist.
  d know that they ought to give up smoking.

5 In the past doctors

  a have taken no interest in hypnotism.
  b have largely ignored hypnotism.
  c have been unaware of the effects of mental stress.
  d have been guilty of a certain lack of enthusiasm.

C *Word study*

Look at this sentence from the text in section A:
For instance, a lady . . . was asked to play an imaginary piano. (ll. 15–16)

For instance is another example of a prepositional phrase, like those in Unit 7, section E. Here are some more, used in context:

Smith was determined to win the prize **at all costs**.
At first sight nothing seemed to have been touched. Then Scott noticed that the safe was open.
The church is **at least** 300 years old.
An off-duty policeman spotted Kershaw **by chance** in a supermarket in Leeds.
I know the words of that song **by heart**.
I didn't know his name, but I knew him **by sight**.
She was surprised that they got on so well, for they had nothing **in common**.
Many of the audience were **in tears** as they came out of the cinema.
I'm sure he broke the window **on purpose**.
George likes the idea of going to live in the country. **On the other hand** he doesn't want to move too far from the office.
By the time we reached the top of the hill, we were all **out of breath**.
I'm afraid you'll have to use the manual typewriter. The electric machine is **out of order**.

Use prepositional phrases from the examples above to replace the words in **bold** *type below so that the meaning of each sentence remains unchanged:*

Example The child was **crying**, because she had lost her pocket money.
The child was **in tears**, because she had lost her pocket money.

1 Their new house must have cost **a minimum of** £60,000.

2 He learnt his speech **so well that he knew all the words.**

3 I'm sure she stood on my foot **intentionally.**

4 **I had a quick look round and** it appeared that nobody had been in the laboratory.

5 I'm afraid you can't use the telephone. It's **not working**.

6 Fred's leg was undoubtedly broken. Phil knew he had to get help before nightfall **no matter how difficult it might be.**

7 The fat man managed to climb onto the roof, but I could see that he was **panting**.

8 If Frank took the job, he would get more money. **However**, he would have to work much longer hours.

9 He met her again at the seaside **without the meeting having been arranged**.

10 We have one interest **that we share**. We both love visiting foreign cities.

D Word study

Study the passage below, then answer the questions.

Accidents and illness

Asthma is an illness. If you were unlucky, you might suffer from asthma. In the winter many people **catch influenza** (flu). They get **a headache, a sore throat** and **a runny nose**, and they **cough** and **sneeze**. If you think you have flu, you should **take your temperature**, using **a thermometer**. If you find that you have a temperature, you should go to bed, keep warm, take some aspirins and drink plenty of liquid.

Bicycle racing is dangerous. Sometimes the riders crash and **break** a leg or an arm. In less serious cases they may **fracture** a bone. If they are **badly injured**, they will be taken to the hospital in **an ambulance**. Before this, however, they will usually receive **first aid**. If someone is injured with a weapon – **stabbed** with a knife or **shot** with a gun – we say he or she has been **wounded**.

Middle-aged men, particularly if they are **unfit** or **overweight**, sometimes suffer from **heart attacks**. It is often said that one of the causes of heart attacks is **stress**. **A psychiatrist** is a doctor who specializes in **treating patients** who are **mentally ill**, or people who have serious problems which they wish to discuss with a doctor. Often these problems are connected with their **relationships** with other people.

1 Mr Digby is fifty-seven years old, overweight and worried. What might happen to him?

2 Describe how you would feel if you had flu.

3 Being a soldier is not always fun. Soldiers are sometimes wounded. Who by?

4 Policemen are given training in first aid. Think of a situation in which a policeman might find this training useful.

5 Think of two things you could stab somebody with.

6 If you were a doctor at a hospital near a ski resort, what sort of injury would you expect to deal with quite often?

7 What would you use to find out if you had a temperature?

8 Mrs Scott is worried. Mr Scott thinks he is Tarzan. What kind of doctor should he see?

E *Focus on grammar:* passive voice 1

In the text a number of examples of the passive voice occur.
Compare the active and passive ways of expressing ideas:

Active	Passive
Doctors sometimes **use** hypnotism . . .	Hypnotism **is** sometimes **used** . . . (l. 26)
The doctor **may ask** him or her to . . .	They **may be asked** to . . . (ll. 20–21)
The hypnotist **asked** a lady to play . . .	. . . a lady . . . **was asked** to play . . . (l. 16)
The hypnotist **will tell** him or her to . . .	. . . he or she **will be told** to . . .
The medical profession **has shown** little interest in the subject . . .	. . . little interest **has been shown** in the subject by the medical profession . . . (ll. 28–29)
Her parents **had forced** her to take piano lessons . . .	. . . she **had been forced** to take piano lessons . . . (l. 18)

Notes When changing a sentence from the active to the passive voice:
a the object becomes the subject of the sentence.
b we use the correct tense of the verb 'to be'+the past participle of the main verb in the active sentence (the tense does not alter).

There are two more sentences in the text which use the passive.
Can you find them?

F Grammar practice

Rewrite the following statements in the passive voice.

Example   The robbers forced the manager to open the safe.
The manager . . .
The manager was forced to open the safe.

1   The young man stabbed the policeman.
The policeman . . .

2   The doctor will tell you to give up smoking.
You . . .

3   I have mended the record player.
The . . .

4   They may ask you to tell your story again.
You . . .

5   Richard had lost the key.
The . . .

6   They told me to come and see you.
I . . .

7   We often find interesting stamps on the letters from abroad.
Interesting . . .

8   They may ask you to show them your passport.
You . . .

Now rewrite the following passive statements in the active voice.

Example   First aid is often given to injured people by policemen.
Policemen . . .
Policemen often give first aid to injured people.

9   She was told to drive to the airport.
They . . .

10   A lot of old films are shown on television.
They . . .

11   The suitcase had definitely been opened.
Someone . . .

12   He was forced to take swimming lessons by his father.
His . . .

13   You will be informed as soon as the results of the test arrive.
They . . .

14   You may be asked to make a short speech.
They . . .

15   He was told to empty his pockets by the policeman.
The . . .

16   My purse has been stolen.
Someone . . .

G *Focus on grammar:* I wish+would/could
I wish+had (past perfect)

Hypnotism might help somebody who is having difficulty in giving up smoking. If you had a friend you thought smoked too much, you might say: 'I wish you would give up smoking.'

Here are some more examples:

I wish Frank would lend me the money.
I wish the weather would improve.
I wish I could get that tape.

In each case the speaker is expressing the hope that something will happen in the future but does not believe that it will.

Compare them with:

I wish you'd (you had) remembered the cream, George.

In this case George forgot the cream. It is now too late to do anything about it.

Here are some further examples:

I wish I hadn't (had not) broken my watch. (But I did, so now I don't know what the time is.)
I wish I'd (I had) posted that letter to the insurance company. (But I didn't, so now it won't go till tomorrow.)

H *Grammar practice*

Suggest the circumstances in which people might make the following remarks:

Example 'Oh, dear. I wish I had brought my glasses.'
Perhaps the speaker is at the theatre and is having difficulty reading the programme because he forgot his glasses.

1 I wish the customs officer hadn't asked me to open my suitcase.

2 I wish you wouldn't smoke so much.

3 I wish I could get a job there.

4 I wish she wouldn't turn the volume up so loud.

5 I wish you would come with me on Saturday.

6 I wish you hadn't told him what I said.

7 I wish we could go back there.

8 I wish Henry hadn't seen that advertisement for weight-lifting equipment.

What might you say in the following circumstances?

9 Your flatmate promised to buy some milk but forgot.

10 A friend of yours has grown a moustache. You don't like it.

11   You ordered ravioli and your friend ordered steak and salad. You don't like the ravioli but the steak looks great.

12   You have finished your meal in the restaurant and you're waiting for the waiter to bring the bill. You are in a hurry.

13   A good friend annoys you by eating apples very noisily.

14   You could have gone by train but you decided to go by car. You are stuck in a traffic jam.

15   Your boy/girlfriend insists on wearing a pair of shabby old shoes 'because they're comfortable'.

I Listening comprehension

Imagine you are one of a party of students on a coach and you are going to visit Windsor Castle. Listen to the guide, then put a tick (√) against the correct answers to the questions. In each case only ONE answer is correct.

1   The first castle was built by
   a   William.
   b   Harold.
   c   Hastings.

2   The first castle was made of
   a   stone.
   b   bricks.
   c   wood.

3   The ticket office is on the
   a   north terrace.
   b   south terrace.
   c   east terrace.

4   The students
   a   must buy their own tickets.
   b   must get their tickets from the guide.
   c   don't need any tickets.

5   Your ticket *doesn't* entitle you to see
   a   the Queen's doll's house.
   b   the Queen's apartment.
   c   the State Apartments.

6   The chapel in the castle is called
   a   St John's.
   b   St George's.
   c   St James's.

7   Students wishing to go to Eton must meet at
   a   one o'clock.
   b   two o'clock.
   c   three o'clock.

8   Those going to Eton will *not* see
   a   the school.
   b   the school chapel.
   c   the pupils.

9   The coach will leave from
   a   the Riverside coach park.
   b   the station coach park.
   c   the bus station.

10   The coach will leave at
   a   5.00.
   b   5.15.
   c   5.50.

J Writing activity

A group of English-speaking students is going to spend a month exploring your country. A friend asks you to come to their hotel and make a short speech welcoming the party, telling them about the public transport system, including details of any 'bargain' tickets, and suggesting one or two interesting places they might like to visit.

Write the speech you would make. You will need 120–180 words.

K Interview

1 *Describe the scene in the picture.*

Where do you think the photograph was taken?
Do you think a race is going to take place, or would you say that it had already been run? Why?
Who do you think the driver is, the young man or the young woman? Give reasons.
What do you think the relationship is between the man and the woman? Say why.

How would you feel if someone close to you regularly took part in a dangerous sport like motor racing?
Would you go and watch? Do you think you might try and persuade them to give it up? Would you want to try it yourself?

Get into groups of three or four. Make a list of up to a dozen dangerous sports and put them in order, with the most dangerous at the top of the list and the least dangerous at the bottom. Give reasons for your choice of order.

2

Application Form

I wish to apply to the Tim Kelly Motor Racing School for race training

Full name..

Address..

Tel no. (Day)............   Date of birth...

Nationality..............   Occupation ....

Previous racing experience ....

Type of race training required. Tick the box of your choice.

☐ Half day Sports Saloon Car.
☐ Full day Sports Saloon Car.
☐ Half day Single Seater Racing Car.
☐ Full day Single Seater Racing Car.

Please give an alternative date for your session, including preference for
a.m./p.m.

First Choice..................   Second Choice ....
☐ Morning Session.   ☐ Afternoon Session.

Work in groups of three. Study this form and ask and answer questions about it.
Use
What......? Who......? Can......? Would......? etc.

L *Writing activity*

A good friend of yours takes part in a dangerous sport as an enthusiastic amateur. You learn that he/she is about to get married. Write a letter, 120–180 words in length, congratulating your friend on his/her engagement but suggesting that the time has come to give up the sport in question.

The following phrases might be useful. (See Unit 8, section L.)

If I were you . . .
If you take my advice, you'll . . .
I think you ought to . . .
Don't you think . . . ?

Test 3

To be done without the aid of a dictionary. No looking back to earlier sections of the book allowed.

Time   1 hour 45 minutes (plus the listening test)

Total possible marks   100

Ratings   70 marks or above: **Good**
55 marks or above: **Fair**
54 marks or less: **A bit disappointing**
45 marks or less: **Very disappointing.** You need to do a great deal of revision.

A   Listen to the news broadcast, then tick (√) whether the answers below are true or false:

		True	False
1	The Prince and Princess said that all young married people had disagreements.		
2	The explosion in the Birmingham flat was caused by an electrical fault.		
3	The Air India jet was searched at Milan airport.		
4	An Oxford student is in hospital after jumping out of her college window.		
5	The Spanish fishing boat was probably fishing too close to the Scottish coast.		
6	The soldier was allowed to use the machine gun during the military exercise.		
7	Dockers at Tilbury went on strike last night.		
8	Some sixty-foot plastic palm trees are being exported to the Persian Gulf.		

8 marks

B   Complete the following sentences by adding one word:

1   Poor Mrs Simpson passed .... when she heard the news. It took her some time to recover.

2   .... to my information you were in Bolton last Tuesday.

3   Mr Rogers checked .... of the hotel and went to the railway station.

4   Everybody .... from me seems to have heard the story.

5   Sally was dead tired. She tried to keep awake, but it was warm in the room and she soon dropped ....

6   .... on a moment, while I make a phone call.

7   I know it was a shock. But you'll soon get .... it.

8   .... to a snowstorm, all trains have been cancelled.

9   It's obvious that Rodney takes .... his mother.

10   Come on. You mustn't .... up now. There's not far to go.

   10 marks

C   *Use a gerund (—ing) or an infinitive, with or without* **to**, *to complete the following sentences:*

1   She's looking forward to (see) her family again.

2   We know that Mackenzie stopped (buy) a newspaper on the way to the station.

3   Martin advised me (come) and see you.

4   When Ron was young he used (like) football very much.

5   The moment he saw the two men Derek stopped (whistle).

6   Do you honestly enjoy (work) there?

7   I'm not used to (eat) a big meal in the middle of the day.

8   Did you remember (turn off) all the lights?

9   I really think you ought (see) a doctor.

10   I don't want a lift thanks. I'd rather (walk).

   10 marks

D   *Finish each of the following sentences in such a way that it means the same as the sentence before it:*

1   I won't go to the concert if you don't come.
     Unless . . .

2   She would feel lost without her radio.
     If she . . .

3   I won't write to her unless she writes to me.
     If she . . .

4   What will you do if the letter doesn't come by Friday?
     Supposing . . .

5   We would probably win the match, but several of our players are injured.
     If several . . .

6   We can put you up if you don't mind sleeping on the sofa.
     Provided that . . .

7   I'd certainly speak to her about it if she was my sister.
     Were . . .

8 I'll buy a melon at the weekend provided that the price doesn't go up.
If . . .

9 I would give you the book if it was mine.
Were . . .

10 Would you really want to become a professional tennis player if you got the chance?
Supposing . . .

20 marks

E *What would you say in the following situations?*

1 Your flatmate has just spilt a bottle of milk.
I wish . . .

2 You are hoping to go out at the weekend, but the weather has been very bad for several days.
I wish . . .

3 Your friend is wondering whether or not to take the job he has been offered. You think he should.
If I . . .

4 Suggest to a friend that you go to the Chinese restaurant.
. . . the Chinese restaurant.

5 Your friend keeps whistling the same tune over and over again. You find this irritating.
I wish . . .

6 You have a new record, but the record player is broken.
I wish . . .

7 Your friend inquires if you'd prefer tea or coffee.
I'd rather . . .

8 Advise a young person to speak to their teacher about something.
I think you . . .

9 Your flatmate is about to go to work, but looks very ill.
If I . . .

10 Complain to your friend about how he wastes his money.
I wish . . .

20 marks

F *Read this report of a business meeting, then write the actual words spoken by the people who attended the meeting.*

Howard asked the sales representatives to give brief reports on the position in their areas.

Graham said that business was not very good in Scotland. Things weren't too bad in the big cities, but in other areas there was very little money about.

Keith agreed that business was very slow in the north, but he thought the new Rainbow dolls would eventually prove very popular.

Simon said he had been selling a lot of Rainbow dolls in the Midlands. People seemed to appreciate the wide range of clothes that were available.

Helen announced that she was going to arrange a special display of the Rainbow range in big stores in her area. She promised to let everyone know if this proved successful.

Howard thanked everyone. He said it was obvious that the Rainbow range was going to be successful. He told the representatives to make sure that all the stores in their areas carried a good stock.

1   Howard:

2   Graham:

3   Keith:

4   Simon:

5   Helen:

6   Howard:

12 marks

G Either

1   *Tell the story of a film you enjoyed.*

or

2   *Describe how people in your country spend Sunday.*
    Write 120–180 words.

20 marks

Unit 10   Instant Shoe Colour

A Reading comprehension

MISS DYLON®
INSTANT
SHOE COLOUR

Made by the makers of the famous DYLON DYES. For further information write to Annette Stevens of our Consumer Advice Bureau.

DYLON INTERNATIONAL LTD.,
LONDON SE26 5HD, ENGLAND
Made in England
Trade Marks Reg'd.
L/SC/357

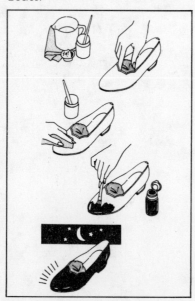

DIRECTIONS
MISS DYLON
For leather and plastic shoes, boots, handbags, belts etc. Not for suede, fabric or rubber. For canvas, dilute Shoe Colour with 25% water. Mix well and apply directly. (Do not use Pre-Conditioner on canvas.) Protect from freezing.

Empty contents of Pre-Conditioner tub into Miss Dylon cap. Slowly add cold water and mix to a smooth creamy paste. Leave for 5-10 minutes. Tightly pack fronts of shoes or legs of boots with newspaper. Wipe clean surface of shoes before conditioning. Re-stir conditioning paste adding more water if required. Using cloth or old toothbrush apply using circular movements to ensure the entire surface has been treated. Special care should be taken to treat creased areas and seams. Wipe surface with clean damp cloth to ensure complete removal of sediment. Allow to dry. Brush out any remaining sediment from creases and stitching with a clean, dry brush.

Shake Shoe Colour bottle well before use. Apply colour evenly with brush. When dry, apply second coat and third if required. Wash brush. Leave overnight, shine with soft cloth before wearing.

For a super shine that's protective too, try Miss Dylon Seal'n Shine after colouring with Shoe Colour.

D.1 Black	D.18 Morning Mist
D.2 Navy Blue	D.19 Silver
D.3 Lunar Blue	D.20 Gold
D.4 Hawaiian Blue	D.21 Roman Purple
D.6 Avocado	D.23 Ming Yellow
D.8 Copacabana	D.24 Red Fox
D.9 Miami Tan	D.25 Cypress Green
D.11 Hot Chocolate	D.26 Dark Brown
D.13 Deep Teak	D.30 Mulberry
D.14 Chianti Red	D.31 Bondi Beach
D.15 Persian Red	D.33 Magnolia
D.16 Pink Tulip	D.34 Burgundy
D.17 White	D.35 Storm Grey

Satin Shoes
Use Dylon multi-purpose dyes. Wash shoes before colouring, leave slightly damp. Pad insides with newspaper. Dissolve contents of Dylon tin in one pint boiling water, stir well. Apply dye solution with old toothbrush using light circular motion, repeat process to obtain deeper shade.

B *Multiple choice questions*

Choose the best answer.

1 You shouldn't use this instant shoe colour

a on leather shoes.
b on canvas shoes.
c on plastic shoes.
d on suede shoes.

2 Before using the conditioner, you should

a mix the colour to a smooth paste.
b clean the outside of the shoes.
c wet the inside of the shoes.
d rub the surface of the shoes with newspaper.

3 You are advised to

a use a weaker solution of colour for canvas shoes.
b shake the shoe colour bottle after using it.
c wipe the shoes with a damp cloth immediately after colouring.
d apply a second coat of shoe colour for rubber shoes.

4 You should

a pad fabric shoes with paper before colouring.
b make sure that creases are filled with sediment.
c dry the shoes with a clean, dry brush.
d let the shoes dry completely before applying more colour.

5 To dye satin shoes you should

a make sure the shoes are dry before colouring.
b mix the dye in cold water before using.
c stuff the shoes with newspaper before colouring.
d use the same shoe colour recommended for suede shoes.

C Word study

The following words, referring to materials used to make shoes, appear in the text:

canvas, **leather**, **plastic**, **rubber**, **satin**, **suede**.

Here are some more materials:

brass	**concrete**	**flour**	**linen**
cardboard	**copper**	**fur**	**plaster**
clay	**cork**	**iron**	**wax**

Work in groups of three or four. See which of the above words you already know between you. Then use an English/English dictionary to find the meaning of any unknown words. Finally, complete the chart below using words from the lists above.

Ball point pens		plastic
Cornflakes packets		....
China cups		....
Some clocks		....
Some water pipes		....
Some ceilings		....
Some ladies' dresses		....
Candles	are made from	....
Some gloves		....
Some sails		....
Some bridges		....
Some coats		....
Some pillowcases		....
Some paving stones		....
Some bathroom floor tiles		....
Bread rolls		

D Word study

Here is a further selection of phrasal verbs. Study them carefully, then do the exercise below.

break down	**fall for**	**put off**
break off	**go off**	**set off**
call off	**look after**	**think up**
come off	**look for**	**wear off**
die away	**make up (for)**	**wear out**

A car may **break down**. The engine stops working, so the car won't move.
The handle of a jug might **break off** if you gave it a knock.
An open-air concert might be **called off** because of bad weather.
If a plan proves successful we can say the plan **came off**.
The sound of music can **die away** as we walk away from the bandstand.
Brenda went to work for a farmer. She **fell for** her boss and married him.
Bombs and shells don't always **go off**. (explode)
Simon's aunt **looked after** him while his mother was in hospital.
The man with the metal detector was **looking for** metal objects on the seashore.
The children couldn't go to the circus, so we're going to take them to see Treasure Island to **make up** for it.
He **put off** going to see the doctor as long as possible.
Early the next morning they **set off** on their journey.
The prisoners spent a lot of time trying to **think up** a way of escaping from the island.
After a while the dye began to **wear off** the shoes, so I had to colour them again.
I'm afraid this skirt is **worn out**. I'll have to throw it away and buy a new one.

Answer these questions, which use phrasal verbs from the list above:

1   Suggest why an opera performance might be called off.

2   What would you do if your car broke down in the middle of a busy street?

3   Suggest why the people next door might ask you to look after their dog.

4   If you had a pullover that was worn out what would you do with it?

5   The captain of the football team thought up a very clever plan, and it came off. What was the result?

6   Judith became a film actress. She fell for her leading man. This was most unfortunate because . . .

7   The shell landed on the cottage and went off with a terrible bang. What was the result?

8   It broke off in my hand while I was trying to unlock the safe and now it's stuck. What is *it* and what is the problem going to be?

9   David couldn't go to the Christmas party because he was sick. To make up we're going to take him . . .

10 Slowly the pain wore off and George began to feel better. Suggest what might have happened.

E Focus on grammar: passive voice 2

Compare the active and passive ways of expressing these facts about the shoe colouring process:

Active	Passive
You **have to add** water to the pre-conditioner.	Water **has to be added** to the pre-conditioner.
You **ought to keep** the dye in a warm, dry place.	The dye **ought to be kept** in a warm, dry place.
You **should shake** the bottle before you **use** the dye.	The bottle **should be shaken** before the dye **is used.**
You **shouldn't have used** that sort of dye on satin shoes.	That sort of dye **shouldn't have been used** on satin shoes.
We **will have used** all this by the weekend.	All this **will have been used** by the weekend.
If you **had shaken** the bottle properly, you **would have achieved** a more professional finish.	If the bottle **had been shaken** properly, a more professional finish **would have been achieved**.

F Grammar practice/Writing activity

You work for the public relations department of a firm that makes insecticides. A customer called Mr Cook has written to complain that after spraying his beans with 'Killit', one of your products, his hair fell out. Mr Cook has admitted that it was very windy on the day he sprayed the beans.
Your chief asks you to deal with the matter. Here are your notes.

Write to the customer. You will find that you use the passive several times:

Dear Mr Cook,

Thank you for your letter of 25th August.

a   We / sorry / learn / that you / suffer / hair-loss.

b   However we / regret / not / accept / responsibility / unfortunate / occurrence.

c   Before / use / 'Killit' spray / customers / ask / read / instructions / carefully.

d   When you / use spray / instructions / bottle / obviously / not followed.

e   It is true / spray / contain / small quantity / arsenic.

f   This fact / clearly / state / bottle.

g Unfortunately / you / guilty / three errors of judgement:

h 1. A much / weak / solution / spray / use.

i 2. The beans / never / spray / such / windy day.

j 3. If you / aware / spray / fall / hair / you / wash / at once.

Although, as stated above, we are unable to accept responsibility for this unfortunate occurrence, we offer our sympathy and hope that your hair will grow again soon.

Yours sincerely,

G *Focus on grammar:* Third conditional/inverted conditional

Read this story:

A little girl was brought into a London hospital suffering from a mysterious illness. She was almost unconscious and growing weaker by the hour. The doctors were unable to decide what was wrong until a nurse, who had been reading a book by Agatha Christie, suggested it might be thallium poisoning. The little girl was losing her hair and she had white lines on her fingernails. Tests were carried out which proved that the nurse was right. The doctors were now in a position to prescribe the correct treatment and the young patient was soon on the mend. But if the nurse **had not been reading** the murder mystery and if Agatha Christie **had not done** her research so thoroughly, the little girl **would** probably **have died**.

When we use the third (or past) conditional, we know that the event being discussed did not happen. It can be used as a means of expressing regret, the wish that circumstances had been different or perhaps that you had behaved differently.

If Agatha Christie had not done her research so thoroughly, the **little girl would . . . have died**. (But Agatha Christie *did* do her research thoroughly, the nurse read the book and the little girl was saved.)

If the nurse had not been reading the book, **she wouldn't have thought** of thallium poisoning. (But she *was* reading the book, so she *did* think of thallium poisoning.)

We can also use the inverted conditional:

Had the little girl not been ill, her parents wouldn't have brought her to the hospital. (But she *was* ill, so they brought her.)

When we wish to express the idea of possibility, we can use **might have** or **might not have** instead of **would have** or **wouldn't have**:

If the little girl's parents had not brought her to London, **she might have died**. (**. . . might not have lived**.)

Had the little girl's parents not brought her to London, **she might have died**.

H Grammar practice

Use the information below to make third conditional sentences.

Example   It rained, so we didn't go for a picnic.
If it hadn't rained, we would have gone for a picnic.
or
Had it not rained, we would have gone for a picnic.

1   They found my keys, so they were able to get into the house.

2   There was a rail strike, so we went by car.

3   She saw the programme about animals being killed, so she became a vegetarian.

4   Her brother didn't see the programme, so he didn't change his eating habits.

5   He was watching television, so he didn't hear the burglars.

6   We didn't put the milk in the fridge, so it went sour.

7   He lied before, so I didn't believe him this time.

8   She was feeling tired, so she didn't dance.

9   The little boy gave the alarm, so the family weren't burnt to death.

10   You weren't listening to the instructions, so you didn't know where to go.

Continue in the same way, but this time practise using **might have** or **might not have** instead of **would have** or **wouldn't have**:

11   He didn't look smart when he went for his interview. He didn't get the job.

12   They lost their way. They didn't arrive in time.

13   You didn't give me your address. I didn't write to you.

14   The horse didn't jump the last fence properly. It didn't win the race.

15   The water was so cold. She didn't go for a swim.

●● I *Listening comprehension*

Tim Gates is planning to stay at a small seaside hotel with some friends. He has an Eastbourne telephone number which he is ringing now.
Listen to the conversation and fill in the information in the list of questions that Tim has prepared. You will hear the conversation twice.

1 and 2 Cost of rooms (including bed and breakfast):

Single: £ ....

Double: £ ....

3 Cost of evening meal: £ ....

4 Time of evening meal: ....

5 Are there showers in the rooms? ....

6 How far is the hotel from the sea? ....

7 Car parking? ....

8 Name of hotel ....

9 Address: ....

....

10 Occupy rooms from: ....

●● J *Communicative practice:* **generalizations**

(I think) people are inclined to . . . (People) tend to . . . . . . seem to be getting . . . _____	Yes, they are, aren't they? Well, perhaps. Yes, they do, don't they? Oh, do you think so? Yes, that's true. Oh, I'm not sure I agree with you.

Model conversations

1 a I think people are inclined to worry too much about their health.

b Yes, they are, aren't they? *or* Well, perhaps.

Work in pairs. Use the phrases in the box to make similar conversations.

worry too much about money eat too much sugar take too many pills watch too much television spend too much money on frozen vegetables and tinned fruit

2 a Scotsmen tend to be quick-tempered.

b Yes, they do, don't they? *or* Oh, do you think so?

Continue working in pairs. Use the phrases in the box to make similar conversations. Then make similar generalizations about other nationalities.

> Italians/talk a lot
> The French/regard food as important
> The Welsh/be small and dark
> Africans/have a great sense of humour
> Americans/learn to drive when they're very young

3 a New flats seem to be getting smaller all the time, don't they?

b Yes, that's true. *or* Oh, I'm not sure I agree with you.

Continue working in pairs. Use the phrases in the box to make similar conversations. Then think of some more generalizations to make to your partner, who must respond suitably.

> films/more violent
> holidays/more expensive
> airports/busier
> blocks of offices/higher
> the weather/worse

K Writing activity

Read the information below about three families. Then, on page 131, study the details of five houses being offered for sale in or near the town of Bedford. Finally, write three paragraphs explaining which house you think would be the best choice for each family. You will need about 65 words for each paragraph.

The Turner family: Mr Turner is about to retire after working for more than forty years in the post office. The Turners own a three-bedroomed house which is worth about £35,000. Now that their family have grown up and left home, it is too large for them. Mrs Turner is having a bit of trouble with her legs.

The Purvis family: Ted Purvis and his wife, Rita, have been married for five years and have two young children. They are living in a rented flat, which is too small, and they are having trouble with neighbours, who say their children are noisy. Ted works for a local builder. He has considerable experience of the building trade, although he is not yet thirty. Rita has a part-time job at a local supermarket. They do not have a lot of capital, but could raise a deposit of £2,000.

The Hart family: Roger Hart is a junior executive with an international business organization. His wife and he have decided to move to Bedford for the sake of their two children's education. The children are aged five and seven. Roger intends to commute to London every day. The Harts have paid ten years of a twenty-year mortgage on a house in London. Roger earns a good salary.

GOLDINGTON GREEN
£25,950

Well-planned 2-bed ground-floor flat enjoying park views and offering entrance hall, lounge, 2 good beds., kitchen, bathroom. Vacant possession.

OAKLANDS ROAD
£48,000

Substantial double bay-fronted semi-detached corner house close to town centre. In need of improvement and modernization, the property provides porch, hall, cloakroom, living room, dining room, drawing room, study, kitchen, 4 bedrooms, bathroom, w.c., large rear garden. Space for garage, subject to planning permission.

PUTNOE
£40,000

Established modern semi-detached home. Entrance hall, lounge, dining room, kitchen, 3 bedrooms, bathroom, separate w.c., full gas radiator central heating, double glazing, garage, gardens.

PUTNOE
£32,500

Mature 2-bedroomed det. bungalow, well positioned and benefiting from reception hall, living room, kitchen, 2 beds., bathroom, gas c.h., garage space and gardens.

GARFIELD STREET
£20,000

Pleasant mid-terraced house in convenient location to the north of the town centre. 2 reception rooms, modern fitted kitchen, 2 bedrooms, first-floor bathroom. West-facing garden. Ideal for first-time buyers. Early vacant possession.

Unit 11 The Japanese Attitude to Holidays

A Reading comprehension

The Japanese Attitude to Holidays

As they travel to their factories and offices on dark, cold winter mornings, workers throughout Europe are cheered by the thought that in a few short months it will be spring; and knowing that spring will in due course be followed by summer, they look forward eagerly to a holiday spent at the
5 seaside perhaps, or in the country. Many firms close down completely for three or four weeks during July or August and even when they remain open it is taken for granted that everybody will enjoy a well-earned break.

In Japan, on the other hand, the situation is a little different. An employee of a big firm in Japan is normally entitled to approximately twenty days paid
10 leave in any one year and he could take them all at once if he wished; in fact Japanese workers are inclined to adopt such a conscientious attitude to their work that they seldom avail themselves of their full holiday allowance. The reasons for this are partly a fear of placing an unfair burden upon the shoulders of one's colleagues and partly the knowledge that to take one's
15 entire holiday entitlement when others did not would probably harm one's chances of promotion.

A survey released recently by the Tokai Bank claims that 90 per cent of male employees working for major companies will not take more than five days off this year, usually for a trip to the seaside, to the country or to the home of a
20 relative. The five days will almost certainly include a Sunday, which would in any case be free. Remember, too, that in Europe the five-day working week is usual, whereas in Japan it is comparatively rare. However, Japanese women, whose career prospects tend to be limited, do not share this worry. Last year some 63 per cent of women took all the holidays to which they were
25 entitled. Nevertheless, it would appear that recent reports of a decline in company loyalty and enthusiasm for work amongst the younger generation of Japanese workers have been greatly exaggerated.

B *Multiple choice questions*

Choose the best answer.

1 European workers going to work

a are aware the spring comes after winter.
b feel very cheerful as they travel to work in winter.
c all look forward to their summer holidays at the seaside.
d cheer when they think of spring.

2 In Europe

a all firms shut down for three or four weeks in the summer.
b the assumption is made that some workers will have a summer holiday.
c everybody enjoys his or her summer holiday.
d all workers expect to get an annual holiday.

3 In Japan

a 90 per cent of male workers will visit the home of a relative during the summer.
b 90 per cent of the staff of the Tokai Bank will take less than five days summer holiday this year.
c 10 per cent of male workers will take more than five days summer holiday this year.
d 10 per cent of those working for the Tokai Bank will visit the seaside this summer.

4 In Japan some workers don't take all the holidays which are due to them because

a they are afraid of their fellow workers.
b they are afraid of losing their jobs.
c they are afraid it might mean other people having to work too hard.
d they are afraid that if they did they might be promoted.

5 Japanese women

a have the same opportunities for promotion as men.
b do not worry about their jobs.
c take all the holidays due to them.
d are more likely to take the holidays due to them than men.

C Word study

Find words or phrases in the text that mean:

1 comforted and encouraged:
2 assumed:
3 deserved holiday:
4 load:
5 allowance:
6 damage:
7 the obtaining of a more responsible job:
8 but in contrast:
9 fairly uncommon:
10 weakening of:

D Word study

The following words are all connected with travel:

travel   trip   excursion   journey   voyage

Complete the following sentences, using these words. Indicate where there is more than one suitable answer:

1 We are going for a .... to the seaside on Sunday.

2 At that time the .... from York to Dover took three days.

3 The doctor said that a long sea .... would do her good.

4 .... is quite expensive in some parts of Europe.

5 Tickets for the .... to Brighton on Saturday cost £5.

Match the following words and definitions:

6 person you know, but not well   a colleague
7 person you work with   b team-mate
8 person who is one of your family   c relation
9 person in the same team as you   d friend
10 person you like and enjoy being with e acquaintance

E Word study

Notice how certain words and phrases are used in the text in section A like signposts, indicating what is to follow:

In Japan, **on the other hand**, . . . (l. 8)
However, Japanese women . . . (l. 22–3)

The phrase **on the other hand**, like the words **but** and **however**, indicates a contrast. **On the other hand** and **however** are better expressions than **but** to use at the beginning of a sentence. This is important in written English.

. . . **whereas** in Japan . . . (l. 22)

The writer could have used **while** or **whilst** equally well. These words also introduce the idea that a comparison is about to be made.

. . . **in fact**, Japanese workers . . . (ll. 10–11)

The use of **in fact** indicates that further, more detailed evidence of information is about to be presented.

Nevertheless, it would appear . . . (l. 25)

We use **nevertheless** to show that a statement is about to be made which may come as something of a surprise, or seem to contradict a previous statement.

Here are two more very useful signpost words:

Fortunately is used to introduce a favourable aspect of a situation.

Unfortunately indicates that we are about to learn of a negative aspect of a situation.

Study each of these expressions used in context:

The habit of making generalizations about people of different nationalities is always a dangerous business. **Nevertheless**, such generalizations are frequently made. We say things like:

Germans always shake hands when they are introduced to a stranger, **whereas** the Japanese give a little bow. Americans, **on the other hand**, nod their heads and say 'Hi'.

Unfortunately the English, like the Americans, are bad at learning foreign languages. **Fortunately, however**, people all over the world speak excellent English.

In fact none of these statements is completely true.

The passage below presents facts about Japanese and European society. *Fill the gaps using* **however, in fact, whereas, nevertheless** *or* **on the other hand**.

The Japanese often work for one firm all their working lives, (1) ....
Europeans expect to change their job several times. (2) ....,
a man who stays in one job too long may be accused of lacking initiative.

Arranged marriages are rare in Europe. (3) .... , they do occur,
particularly in rural communities. In Japan, (4) .... , arranged
marriages are still common.

F Focus on grammar: clauses of result

Note the use of **such** *in this sentence:*

Japanese workers are inclined to adopt **such** a conscientious attitude to their work **that** they seldom avail themselves of their full holiday allowance.

Such is an adjective, so it is used with a noun:

It was **such** awful **tea that** we couldn't drink it.

So is an adverb and is therefore used with an adjective or an adverb:

The tea was **so awful that** we couldn't drink it.
She took the news **so calmly that** I wondered if she'd understood.

Too and **enough** are adverbs. Therefore, like **so**, they are used with adjectives or adverbs:

The curry was **too hot** for me to eat.
Unfortunately the doctor didn't get there **quickly enough** to give her treatment.

Look at some more examples:

It's **such** a big **car that** it must be expensive to run.
The car goes **so fast** that it must use a lot of petrol.
The car is **too big** for us. That's why we're selling it.
The car is **big enough** to take you and your family and all the luggage.

G Grammar practice

Complete each of the following sentences in such a way that it means exactly the same as the sentence before it.

Example   It was too dark to see anything.
It was not . . .
It was not light enough to see anything.

1   It was so late that nothing could be done till morning.
It was too . . .

2   That restaurant is so expensive that we can't afford to eat there.
That is such . . .

3   The vegetables were too salty to eat.
The vegetables were so . . .

4   She arrived too late to get a seat.
She didn't . . .

5   It's so windy that it'll be dangerous to take a boat out.
It's too . . .

6   The coffee is so nice that I think I'll have another cup.
It's such . . .

7   It was too hot for her to lie in the sun for long.
It was so . . .

8 This book is so interesting that I'm going to buy a copy.
This is . . .

9 It was too cold to swim in the sea.
It wasn't . . .

10 The map is so complicated that you can easily lose your way.
It's such . . .

H Focus on grammar: have got
have got to
get/have something done

Have got
Got is often used with the verb **have**, particularly in spoken English, without changing the meaning of **have**.

Have they **got** any children?   Do they have any children?
Yes, they**'ve got** two children.   Yes, they have two children.
I **have**n't **got** any money with me.   I don't have any money with me.
At that time I **had**n't **got** a car.   At that time I didn't have a car.

Have got to
We often use the expression **I've got to** as an alternative to **I have to.**
Got to can be used in the present and the past like this:

Have you **got to**?   Do you have to? (Must you?)
I've **got to**.   I have to. (I must.)
I haven't **got to**.   I don't have to. (I needn't.)
Had you **got to**?   Did you have to?
I'd **got to**.   I had to.
I hadn't **got to**.   I didn't have to.

Have you **got to** go to the bank?
You've **got to** pay before you go in.
I'd **got to** give her something.
She hadn't **got to** go to the party.

Get/have something done
Get and **have** are also used with an object+the past participle to indicate that the subject hired somebody to do a job for them:

I usually $\left\{ \begin{array}{l} \textbf{get} \\ \textbf{have} \end{array} \right\}$ my hair cut at that shop.
I usually pay the expert in that shop to cut my hair.

We're $\left\{ \begin{array}{l} \textbf{getting} \\ \textbf{having} \end{array} \right\}$ new windows fitted.
We're going to pay somebody to fit new windows.

We're going to $\left\{ \begin{array}{l} \textbf{get} \\ \textbf{have} \end{array} \right\}$ the car re-sprayed.
We're going to pay somebody to re-spray the car.

They $\left\{ \begin{array}{l} \textbf{got} \\ \textbf{had} \end{array} \right\}$ their roof repaired.
They hired a man to repair their roof.

I Grammar practice

*Read the conversation between Liz and Keith and replace the phrases in **bold** type with expressions using **get** or **got**:*

Saturday morning. Keith comes down to the kitchen in his dressing-gown. Liz is fully dressed and is just finishing her breakfast.

Keith	You were up early this morning.
Liz	Yes, (1) **I have to** go into the office.
Keith	But it's Saturday.
Liz	I'm sorry about that, dear, (2) **I have to** see a client.
Keith	On Saturday?
Liz	Poor Mr Potter. (3) **He has** awful problems. His wife's run away with his best friend and he wants a divorce.
Keith	Are you taking the car?
Liz	Yes, I am. (4) **Do you have** the keys by the way?
Keith	Yes. They're upstairs. (5) **I was going to ask the mechanic to change that wheel** this morning.
Liz	Then you can (6) **ask the mechanic to change the wheel** this afternoon, can't you, dear? I'll be back by twelve.
Keith	I'll be busy this afternoon. (7) **I must** go and see about those tickets for the concert.
Liz	The car place is open on Sunday morning. (8) You can see about **changing the wheel** then. (9) **Do you have to** go out this morning?
Keith	Er . . . no . . . I just want a nice, quiet, peaceful morning. Why?
Liz	(10) **We have** a chicken in the fridge, but we need some potatoes, some carrots and some bread.
Keith	O.K. See you about twelve . . .

J Grammar practice

*Practise using **have something done**. Write your answers.*

Think of something you might have done to:

1	a pair of shoes	5	your hair
2	a tooth	6	a piano
3	a pair of trousers	7	a pair of scissors
4	your eyes		

Finally, answer this:

8 Last year the President died. Now his portrait hangs alongside the portraits of all the other past presidents. What did he have done before he died?

K Listening comprehension

Ray Allen has a morning radio programme called *Elevenses*. Once a week Judy Stokes, who has written a number of cookery books, gives listeners a recipe. *Listen to today's recipe and answer the questions below:*

The ingredients are:

1 ....

2 ....

3 ....

4 The first thing to do is:..

5 The second thing to do is: ....

6 The third thing to do is:..

7 What do you do with the boiling water? ....

8 When do you add the lemon juice from the refrigerator? ....

L Writing activity

The recipe in section K is a real one, and you can use it to make delicious lemonade. If necessary listen to it once more, then, in your own words, write instructions for making the lemonade.
You will need 80–120 words. Begin like this:

To make this lemonade you will need . . .

M Interview

Little Old Lady Battered to Death for £5

Postmaster Shot by Armed Raider

American Aircraft Hi-jacked by 3 Armed Men

Policeman Knifed in Sweet Shop Robbery

Burglar Shoots Man Aged 73

Innocent Bystander Knocked Unconscious by Police say Witnesses

1 *Look at the headlines above. How do you feel about each one?*

Would you agree that violence is increasing in our society? If so, why do you think this is?

Do you think newspapers and television give too much publicity to violent crime? If so, why do you think they do this?

English policemen don't usually carry guns. What do you think about this? Have you any idea why they don't carry guns?

Do you believe that more severe punishment might reduce the level of crime generally?

What sentences would you suggest for people found guilty of the following crimes?

a A bank robbery where staff were threatened with guns, £50,000 was stolen, but nobody was hurt.

b Killing a policeman while trying to escape from the scene of a crime.

c Mugging a woman in the street, knocking her to the ground and stealing her handbag which contained £10.

d Stealing a car for use in a robbery.

e Attacking supporters of a visiting football team, using sticks and bottles as weapons.

f Attacking a bus-conductor after an argument about fares, injuring him so severely that he needed hospital treatment.

2 Graph showing the number of unemployed persons and the number of burglaries reported to the police in the town of Shelbourne between 1976 and 1985.

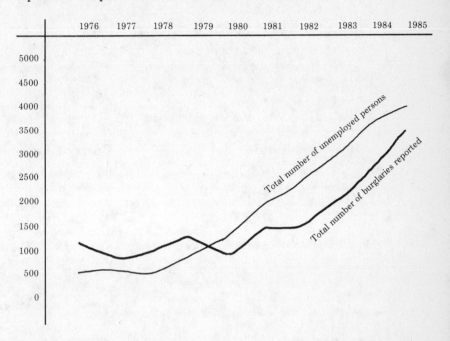

Work in pairs.

a Discuss what the graph shows.

b Comment on what the graph shows for 1979–80 and 1985.

c What conclusions can you draw about the relationship between unemployment and burglary?

N *Writing activity*

Write 120–180 words on 'Violent crime in our society'.

Write three paragraphs. In the first give an example of a recent violent crime that has been in the news. In the second write about the causes of such crimes. In the third suggest what steps might be taken to combat violent crimes such as the one you mention in your opening paragraph.

Unit 12 Financial Advice for Foreign Students Coming to Britain

A Reading comprehension

Financial Advice for Foreign Students Coming to Britain

So you're coming to Britain to study. You're probably going to live with an English family. Have you thought about money?

The last thing you should do is carry large amounts of cash about with you and it's not playing the game with your landlady to keep a pile of notes hidden under your mattress.

If you're wise you'll bring traveller's cheques rather than cash, but there's no reason why you shouldn't open a bank account.

Deposit Accounts

A deposit account is really designed for people who wish to save money. However, this type of account can be very useful for foreign students too.

How much do I need to open an account?

You can start with as little as £1, but most foreign students would probably start by paying in the bulk of the traveller's cheques they have brought over.

How do I pay in?

The bank will give you a paying-in book which will provide you with a record of your deposits, and of course money from a foreign bank can be paid direct into your account.

Will my money earn interest?

Yes, interest is calculated on your account each day and every six months the interest is added to the total sum in your account.

Can I withdraw money easily?

You can take part or all of the money out of your account whenever you wish.

How do I open a deposit account?

No problem. You just fill in a simple form and hand it in at the branch where you'd like to open the account, together with your initial deposit.

Current Accounts

If you're staying in Britain for longer than six months you might like to open a current account. In this case you would be provided with a cheque book, which makes sending money through the post easy, and if you have a current account, you can arrange for bills to be paid by the bank.

How do I open a current account?

Go to the branch where you wish to open the account. You will be asked to fill in a form giving your name, address and certain other personal details. The bank will also ask you for a suitable means of identification (your passport will do nicely) and the name of a referee resident in Britain. It usually takes about ten days to open an account and arrange for a cheque book to be printed with your name.

How will I know how much money I have in my account?

The bank will send you regular statements of account. In any case you can always go into your bank and ask the cashier to let you know your balance.

How much will all this cost?

It varies slightly from bank to bank, but in general you won't have to pay anything, provided that you keep a credit balance of at least £100 in your account.

Foreign students enrolled for full-time courses in Britain should ask at their school, college or university for a letter of introduction to a local bank, where they will receive a friendly and courteous welcome.

B *Multiple choice questions*

Choose the best answer.

1 It's not fair to the landlady of a foreign student for him/her to

a keep a lot of traveller's cheques in his/her room.
b keep a lot of cash in his/her room.
c carry large amounts of cash about with him/her.
d carry large amounts of traveller's cheques about with him/her.

2 Deposit accounts

a are intended for use by foreign students.
b are intended for use by people wishing to put money by.
c are unsuitable for use by foreign students.
d are unsuitable for use by people wishing to accumulate capital.

3 Whenever you pay money into your deposit account

a an entry will automatically appear in your paying-in book.
b you must take your paying-in book with you to the bank.
c the bank will insist that an entry is made in your paying-in book.
d it is only sensible to take your paying-in book with you to the bank.

4 a It's more complicated to open a current account than a deposit account.
b It's less easy to open a deposit account than a current account.
c It doesn't take so long to open a current account as it does to open a deposit account.
d It's usually quicker to open a current account than it is to open a deposit account.

5 If you open a current account

a only a small amount of interest will be paid on your money.
b the interest you receive will depend on how much money you have in your account.
c the amount you have to pay will depend on the amount of money in your account.
d you will only have to pay the bank if your balance falls below £10.

C Word study

This is a test exercise designed to give you practice in Question 1 of the Use of English paper. Fill in each of the numbered blanks in the following passage. Use only one word in each space.

When I left school I looked (1) .... for a job and I (2) .... found one working in a newsagent's shop. (3) .... I didn't have to deliver papers, I soon got (4) .... know the customers who placed a regular order (5) .... a particular newspaper or magazine, (6) .... they came into the shop every day or at (7) .... once a week. However, it was only when the manager went (8) .... holiday (9) .... I was given the job of putting aside these special orders. (10) .... the Monday morning I arrived much earlier (11) .... usual. Outside the shop there was a huge pile (12) .... newspapers (13) .... tied together. I had to cut the string, sort out the various newspapers and then take out the special orders (14) .... the different newspapers were put out for sale. (15) .... each case I had to write the customer's name on the newspaper. But it all took much longer than I had imagined it would. By eight o'clock there was a long queue (16) .... the shop, and impatient customers were rattling the door handle. (17) .... I had to open the shop (18) .... before I was ready. That day I had four separate arguments with customers (19) .... specially ordered newspapers had been sold before (20) .... arrived to collect them.

D Word study: items that can cause confusion

This section contains a number of items which frequently appear in the exam and can cause difficulties. *Study them carefully.*

1   Oh, my purse has been stolen.
Then **you'd better** report it at once.
(Then I advise you to report it at once.)

We can use **had better** in any person (I'd better, you'd better, he'd better, we'd better, they'd better).
It has the meaning of **ought to**, and a negative form: **'d better not.**

2   Would you like to go out this evening?
I'd rather stay at home.
(I'd prefer to stay at home.)

We can use **would rather** in any person (I'd rather, you'd rather, he'd rather, we'd rather, they'd rather).
It has the meaning of **'d prefer to**, and a negative form: **'d rather not**.

3 **Do you happen to** to know which platform the Oxford train leaves from?
You don't happen to know which platform the Oxford train leaves from, **do you**?
(Which platform does the Oxford train leave from?)

This is a polite way of asking questions and can also be used in the past:
Did you happen to see that film about spiders?
You didn't happen to go to the bank this morning, **did you**?

4 **I don't suppose** you have change for a pound, **do you**?
(Have you got change for a pound?)

This is another polite way of asking a question.
It is an alternative to: **Do you happen to . . .?** or **You don't happen to . . . , do you?**

5 **I suppose** Veronica will be at the party.
(I expect Veronica will be at the party.)

Depending on the way it is said, this remark, beginning **I suppose**, could indicate a **dislike** of Veronica or a wish that she **wasn't** coming to the party.

6 **I doubt whether** George will have a key.
I doubt if George will have a key.
(I don't think George will have a key.)

I doubt whether/I doubt if can be used to introduce comments about the past, present or future:

I doubt whether he is enjoying his dinner.
I doubt if he knew anything about it.

The verb **doubt** can also be used in the past:

Sally told me **she doubted whether** we would get tickets.

7 The firemen **prevented him from** enter**ing** his own house.
(The firemen stopped him from going into his own house.)

The verb **prevent** is listed in Unit 5 with other verbs that usually take a gerund. It can be used in all tenses and is nearly always followed by **from+-ing**, a noun or a pronoun.

Anyway, the smoke **would have prevented him from getting** into the house.
By removing the gas cylinders, the firemen **prevented an explosion**.

8 Renata **suggested going** to the disco.
(Renata proposed that we should go to the disco.)

Suggest is also listed in Unit 5 amongst the verbs normally taking a gerund, but it is worth noting two alternative ways of using it:

Renata **suggested that we should** go to the disco.
Renata **suggests we go** to the disco.

Note that **suggest** can *never* be followed by **to**.

*Complete the following conversation, replacing the phrases in **bold** type with items from the examples on pages 144–5. Point out where alternative answers are acceptable.*

Mrs Gilbert is in the sitting-room. Beside her on a small table is a tray with a pot of tea, cups and saucers, chocolate biscuits and a currant cake. The door opens and her daughter Barbara enters.

Mrs Gilbert	Hello dear. Come in and have some tea.
Barbara	Thanks.
Mrs Gilbert	A chocolate biscuit?
Barbara	I think (1) **I'd prefer to** have a piece of cake.
Mrs Gilbert	Of course. Help yourself. What time are you planning to leave for London?
Barbara	(2) **I don't think** Bob will get here till about five. (3) **Do you know** if there's a train that leaves about six?
Mrs Gilbert	There's a timetable beside the telephone, but it may be out of date. (4) **I'd advise you to** ring the station and check. Are you staying with Bob's sister tonight?
Barbara	No, she (5) **thought it would be a good idea for us to** spend the night there, but it's a long way from the airport, so we're going to a hotel.
Mrs Gilbert	(6) **I don't expect** you've heard anything from Frank?
Barbara	I didn't really expect to.
Mrs Gilbert	There was nothing (7) **to stop him** writing to wish you good luck. Still, (8) **I expect** he was a bit upset when you decided to marry Bob rather than him.
Barbara	Yes. I think I'll go and ring the station.

E Focus on grammar: used to+infinitive used to+gerund

Used to *as a past form*

People say that your schooldays are the happiest days of your life. I'm not sure that's true. **I didn't use to dislike** school particularly, but **I used to worry** a great deal about silly things, like homework, and **I didn't use to like** algebra. That was because I was bad at it, of course. However, I had a lot of friends and **I used to enjoy** games very much.

Used to+infinitive can be used in any person, but only in the past. It always refers to events which are completely finished:

Victor **used to live** in that ordinary little house. (But when he became famous he moved to a flat in Chelsea.)

There **used to be** an old-fashioned bakery there. (But now there's a car park.)

The forms: **Did you use to** like school dinners?
                I **used to** hate school dinners.
                I **didn't use to** like school dinners.

Used to meaning *accustomed to*

Arnold's mother is talking to Arnold's fiancée:

'Now my dear, a word in your ear. Arnold is a nice lad and I hope you'll be very happy together, but **he's used to being waited on**. You must remember that Arnold is my youngest child and he has three older sisters. They've spoilt him. **He's used to having** his own way about everything. **He's not used to doing** a thing for himself. So you're going to have to train him right from the start to take his share of responsibility.'

Arnold's fiancée, who works full-time, smiles sweetly. 'I'll train him all right. Arnold **will soon get used to doing** his share of the household tasks.'

Meanwhile poor old Arnold is thinking romantic thoughts about how nice it will be to be married.

This form of **used to** can be used in any person and in any tense. It is followed by a gerund, a noun or a pronoun.

I'm used to walking to work.
Come on in. The water's not really cold. **You'll soon get used to it**.
The Italian, **who was used to playing** on clay, found the grass court very fast.
My dear, **you would never get used to the heat**. It's indescribable.

F *Grammar practice*

Once upon a time Red Indians rode across the prairie hunting buffalo. Eskimos built igloos and fished through holes in the ice. Amazonian Indians shot monkeys with poisoned darts. A few Amazonian Indians remain, but sadly their numbers are fast declining. Some Red Indians still live on reservations. Others wear smart business suits and work in the city. Modern Eskimos listen to transistor radios, eat tinned food and drink Pepsi-Cola.

Then there were the Stone Age people and the Aztecs, who have simply disappeared.

Work in groups of three or four. Take any of the people in the passage about which you have some knowledge. Think of the lives they led and consider their

homes   clothes   food   weapons   tools   habits   religious beliefs.

Make a list of the things they used to do.

Then imagine that circumstances forced a family group of these people to come and live in a modern city. Make a list of the things they would have to get used to doing and using.

Compare your lists with those of the other members of the class.

G *Focus on grammar:* future continuous future in the past

Future continuous

Alan and Sonia had been pen-pals for nearly four years. Now, at last, they were going to meet. Sonia was coming in to Heathrow airport on flight SR2087. Once more she glanced at Alan's letter. He had written:

I'll be wearing grey trousers and a blue jacket, with a white rose in my buttonhole.

Sonia had written to him too:

I shall wear my pink coat and skirt, and **I'll be carrying** a copy of *Paris Match* under my arm.

The forms: **Will you be using** the car this afternoon?
        Yes, **I'll be using** it this afternoon, I'm afraid, but **I won't be using** it tomorrow.

We use the future continuous in very much the same way as we use the present continuous as a future, but sometimes there is a clear difference.

Compare: We're buying a new house.

> Here the implication is that the house has been chosen, an offer has been made and negotiations are well advanced.

> **We'll be buying** a new house.

> This is the kind of remark made by someone who has just won a large sum of money in a lottery. The implication is that a decision has been made to buy a new house but that no action has yet been taken. The family hasn't looked at any houses.

Will you be talking to George some time this week?
I won't be taking that job at the tea-room after all.
How will you be coming on Saturday?
We'll be coming by car.

The future continuous is also used for making predictions:

By 1990 children **will be learning** from computers instead of teachers.

Future in the past

Rodney was short of money. With much regret he had decided that he must sell his beloved MG sports car. Alice was keen to buy the car, but she had borrowed money from the bank to pay for the furniture in her flat. Alice said:

In six months **I'll have paid off** the loan to the bank. Then I'll be able to buy your car.

Rodney shook his head and replied:

I'm afraid I can't wait that long. By then **I'll have sold** the car to someone else.

We use the future in the past when talking about an event which we expect to take place *between* now and a stated future time or *during* the stated period.

By next June, **I will have worked** for the firm for five years.
In six months' time the election **will have taken place**. We may have a new government.
The central heating system is very old. By the time he decides to get it overhauled, **they'll have stopped** making the spare parts.

You may find this table useful:

By	1999 next June this time next week the time X happens	Y will have happened.
In	three years' a fortnight's time, a few days'	

H Grammar practice

Complete each of the following sentences, using either the future continuous or the future in the past, so that it means exactly the same as the sentence before it:

1 They are selling their house in the next few months.
They'll . . .

2 He will be dressed in a dark grey suit and a red tie.
He'll . . .

3 We believe he's going to make the decision by the end of the month.
We think he'll . . .

4 You're coming by car next week, aren't you?
You'll . . .

5 We think all the food will be eaten by the scouts by Saturday.
We think the scouts . . .

6 John isn't playing tomorrow, I'm afraid.
John won't . . .

7 I'm certain the letter has arrived at her house by now.
I'm sure she'll . . .

8 I expect we'll see you soon, then.
We'll . . .

Now answer the next two questions as truthfully as possible:

9 What do you think you **will be doing** at this time on Sunday?

10 Think of something which **will have happened** by the end of the month.

I Writing activity

Mr Carlton is having his house redecorated. He has just got home from work and he is talking to Mr Green, the foreman.

Complete the parts of the dialogue which are blank.

Mr Carlton	Hello Mr Green. It's been a lovely day. How (1) . . . ?
Mr Green	Oh, we've been getting on pretty well, sir.
Mr Carlton	When (2) . . . ?
Mr Green	We should have finished the front by the weekend. We've still got to put the top coat on the front door, but as you can see, all the brickwork's finished.
Mr Carlton	Yes, it looks nice. Have you (3) . . . ?
Mr Green	Yes, sir. Jack's been working round the back. He's been burning off the old paint, preparing the woodwork . . .
Mr Carlton	When (4) . . . ?
Mr Green	As soon as Jack's finished. There are still one or two cracks to be filled before we can actually start painting. But . . . er . . . we should be able to make a start tomorrow.
Mr Carlton	Have (5) . . . ?
Mr Green	No, the woodwork seems to be in a pretty good state. The only bit of rotten wood we've found so far is that step below the French windows, but we can easily renew that.
Mr Carlton	Are (6) . . .?
Mr Green	Yes, but we'll need the long ladder to get up to that gutter. You want it painted black, don't you, sir?
Mr Carlton	Yes, that's what we agreed. So when (7) . . . ?
Mr Green	Well, of course it depends on the weather, but if it stays nice, we should have finished the whole job in about another fortnight.
Mr Carlton	Oh, that's (8) . . .
Mr Green	Yes, sir. Thank you, sir.

J *Listening comprehension*

Listen to Eddie Walker's radio guide to what's on in London today. Then answer the questions below. You will hear the information twice.

1 Which station is particularly convenient for Petticoat Lane Market?

2 Where can the Metropolitan Police Band be heard today?

3 What is the name of the famous English writer who is mentioned?

4 What sort of music can be heard in the Horniman Gardens?

5 Whose work can be seen at the Hayward Gallery?

6 What game will be played at the Guy's Hospital sports ground?

7 What will people be able to eat in Battersea Park?

8 What entertainment will there be at the Crystal Palace Concert Bowl, apart from the music?

Discussion

Details were given of eight events. Working individually, make a list of these and put them in order of preference with the event you would most like to attend at the top and the one you would least like to attend at the bottom.

Then work in groups of four or five and discuss the reasons for your choice.

K *Interview*

1 *Work in pairs. Look at the photograph, then answer the questions on the next page.*

a What time of year is it? How do you know?
b Describe the people in the photograph.
c Where do you think they are?
d How do you think the woman is feeling?
e What about the man? How do you know?
f What do you think they might do soon?
g Do you think the man looks bored?
h Do you ever feel bored?
i What do you find boring?
j Can you think of any particular occasions when you felt very bored? Tell your partner about them.

2 *Read this short text about a day out:*

It was awful really. I know I shouldn't grumble, but it was so hot and there was a huge crowd there. Then the children couldn't stand the noise. Some of those planes are terribly noisy; and finally, when we wanted to leave, it took nearly an hour and a half to get away. There were so many cars and of course the road you have to go along is only a little country lane really. We didn't get home till after 8 o'clock and the children were dead tired. I'll never go again.

a Would you expect to hear these words spoken or find them written down? Give reasons for your answer.

What can you say about the speaker/writer?
Where do you think he/she went? What happened there?

b Can you remember any specially successful/unsuccessful trips of this sort?
Say what made them successful/unsuccessful.

L *Writing activity*

Write 120–180 words on 'Things that bore me'.

If you have problems thinking of ideas, here is a suggestion as to how you might plan your essay. Write three paragraphs.

a Think of three things that bore you, such as *people talking about their health, the good old days, sport, certain jobs you have to do.*

b Choose the most boring thing and write about this in your *last* paragraph.

c Use your other two ideas for paragraphs one and two.
You could start like this:

I quite like . . ., but I find . . . very boring . . .

Test 4

To be done without the aid of a dictionary. No looking back to earlier sections of the book allowed.

Time	1 hour 30 minutes
Total possible marks	90
Ratings	65 marks or above: **Good** 50 marks or above: **Fair** 49 marks or less: **A little disappointing** 40 marks or less: **Very disappointing.** You need to do a great deal of revision.

A

Read the text, then choose the best answers to the questions on page 155:

Having spent most of the winter gazing at the garden from inside the house because the weather has been so dreadful, you've probably noticed how dull and dreary your curtains are looking. A new look is just the thing to cheer you up and give the house a facelift . . . Or perhaps it's a task you've been putting off, dismissing the beautiful curtain effects you see in glossy magazines as something only professional designers could tackle.

Yet with very little effort, you could give yourself a new outlook on life and a lovely looking room, simply by popping down to your local department store or DIY shop and picking up a new curtain track or pole.

Harrison Drape have come up with a whole range of clever ideas that make hanging stylish curtains as easy as putting up a picture. The new tracks and poles come in a wide range of styles with full instructions and are easy to fix.

You should always make the track or pole your starting point when considering curtain styles. There's one to suit every type of window and it's from here you will need to measure when calculating how much fabric you will need. There are various things you can do to improve the look of your windows. If you have a window that is too small, for example, you can make it look wider if you extend the curtains beyond the frame on either side and use tie-backs to let in the maximum amount of light.

There are lots of ways you can transform even the dullest and most difficult window. Bay windows can be attractive, but what a headache they are for hanging curtains. However they shouldn't give you any trouble if you use an easy-bend **Adaptatrak,** a PVC track which bends easily round curves. It not only performs perfectly. It looks perfect too, and can be painted any colour you like to co-ordinate with the rest of your room design. It is little finishing touches like co-ordinating the edging on curtains and cushions, or matching your curtains to your wallpaper that can make your room design something special.

If you would like further ideas and inspiration Harrison Drape are offering a free colour booklet called *The Art of Window Dressing* which shows their complete range of tracks and poles and gives useful advice on choosing tracks, measuring and fitting.

For your free copy of the booklet send a stamped (23p) addressed envelope (at least 9in×7in) to: **Free Booklet Offer, The Marketing Dept., Harrison Drape Curtain Tracks,** P.O. Box 233, Bradford Street, Birmingham.

1 This article probably appeared in a magazine

a in the autumn.
b in the summer.
c around Christmas time.
d around Easter time.

2 Harrison Drape manufacture

a curtains of various types.
b ideas for interior design.
c equipment connected with curtains.
d window frames.

3 The article suggests that

a it is very difficult to fit new curtains yourself.
b people should look at glossy magazines to get ideas.
c it will cost you very little to fit new curtains.
d people are nervous about fitting new curtains themselves.

4 a Bay windows are usually dull and difficult.
  b Curtains hanging in a bay window get damaged easily.
  c It is difficult to fit curtains in a bay window.
  d Curtains always look good in a bay window.

5 To obtain a copy of the booklet you could send an envelope measuring

a 9½in.×7½in.   **c** 8in.×7in.
b 5in.×3in.   **d** 7in.×5in.

10 marks

B *Fill each of the numbered spaces in the following passage. Use only* **one** *word in each space.*

Professional ballroom dancers (1) .... start their careers when they are very young. (2) .... they progress through the ranks of the amateurs until they are competing in national or international championships. Wendy reckons that she and (3) .... present partner, Tony, put (4) .... approximately fourteen hours of practice (5) .... week. She works (6) .... a hairdresser and started dancing (7) .... when she was sixteen. She has had three partners. Her first didn't grow as quickly as she did and, as she (8) .... it, a short fat man dancing with a tall, thin lady (9) .... doesn't look right. Her second partner became upset when they failed to (10) .... the final of a regional competition, blamed her for their (11) .... of success, and walked out. She and Tony have been dancing (12) .... for just (13) .... eighteen months. Tony has a factory job (14) .... he says is boring and repetitive (15) .... pays reasonably well. He is two years younger (16) .... Wendy and they were (17) .... to one (18) .... by their dancing teacher. (19) .... they haven't won any prizes yet Wendy feels sure that it's only a (20) .... of time.

20 marks

C *The words in **bold** type in the margin can be used to form words that fit suitably in the blank spaces. Fill each space in this way.*

Example

treat

I think he was very unfairly *treated* ....
I think the *treatment* he received was unfair.

arrange **1** All the .... have been made for the handing over of the prisoners.

identify **2** He had no way of .... himself, so I refused to cash the cheque, sir.

deliver **3** We shall be making a .... in your area on Monday.

contain **4** The drugs were hidden in a metal .... labelled 'powdered milk'.

calculate **5** If my .... are correct, the bomb will not go off for another three hours.

exaggerate **6** You must allow for a certain amount of .... in Turner's account of what happened.

shoot **7** Jackson was .... in an amusement arcade in Soho last June.

vary **8** There is a considerable .... in the average temperature, according to the season.

freeze **9** Last winter the lake ....

take **10** I'm sorry. I .... it for granted you'd be staying to lunch.

10 marks

D *Finish each of the following sentences in such a way that it means the same as the sentence before it:*

1 I've cleaned the gas fire in the front room.
The . . .

2 Please don't make such long telephone calls.
I'd rather . . .

3 Did you have to tell Doris what I said?
Had you . . .

4 They told her that her purse had been found.
She . . .

5 Why don't you take it back to the shop?
I suggest . . .

6 'I don't think I'll come to the party,' said Jean.
Jean doubted . . .

7 You didn't give me the key, so I couldn't get in.
If you . . .

8 He spoke so quietly that I couldn't hear him.
He didn't . . .

9   They might ask you to go to the police station.
You . . .

10   The coffee was so sweet that I couldn't drink it.
The coffee was too . . .

20 marks

E   *Complete the following sentences with a suitable form of* **go***. You may need more than one word:*

1   I've stopped .... to the club myself.

2   She wondered where Daniel ....

3   You look ill. I wish you .... to see a doctor.

4   I'd rather not .... shopping till tomorrow.

5   I don't want to prevent you ....

5 marks

F   *Complete the following sentences with a suitable form of* **used***. You may need more than one word:*

1   If you come to Africa, you will have to .... living in a very hot climate.

2   Elizabeth .... like onions, but now she does.

3   I'm afraid I'm spoilt. I'm .... travelling first class.

4   Peter .... live in Canada. That's why he speaks like that.

5   Goodness, I (never) .... driving on the left-hand side of the road.

5 marks

G *Study the details of four hotels on Greek islands. Imagine you are a travel agent. Recommend the most suitable holiday for:*

a Mr and Mrs Austin. They are business people in their forties. They have no children and are obviously not short of money.

b Mr and Mrs Skinner. They are in their thirties. They have two children, aged ten and seven, and Mr Skinner does not appear to earn a large salary.

Give reasons for your choice. You will need about 50 words for each recommendation.

The hotels: prices include air transport to and from Greece, bed and breakfast in the accommodation, airport taxes and transfers. There is a 10 per cent discount for children.

Pension Zephyros – Karpathos

This small pension on the harbour front and above the family general store offers twin rooms with shared facilities. Ideal for those looking for an inexpensive holiday. The island of Karpathos is the most remote and the least visited by tourists. If you want a simple holiday Karpathos can offer you a unique experience.
2 weeks: £210 per person.

Kamelia Hotel – Kos

Small, family-run C class hotel, pleasantly set among orange trees, 150 metres from the beach. The hotel has a breakfast area and lounge. Kos is a charming island. The town is spacious and elegant with wide, palm-lined avenues and a seafront served by a selection of tavernas.
2 weeks: £280 per person

Hotel Diana – Crete

Situated 5 minutes' walk from the famous harbour of Agios Nikolaos. The hotel is central and offers a choice of rooms with private or shared facilities. Crete is the largest and most southerly island. The scenery is dramatic, with mountains dotted with small villages.
2 weeks: £300 per person.

Spetse Hotel – Spetse

This A class hotel is situated 10 minutes' walk from the town. It has a palm-thatched beach restaurant. The bedrooms have private showers, W.C. and terrace. At night Spetse really comes alive. The tavernas are too numerous to mention, serving anything from pizzas to local dishes such as *moussaka*.
2 weeks: £360 per person.

20 marks

Appendix: phrasal verbs

ask after enquire about
back out of fail to do something that has been agreed
back up support someone
break down stop working (e.g. an engine)
●lose control of one's emotions
break in enter a building using force
break off become separated from
break up separate (lovers or a married couple)
bring off succeed in difficult circumstances
bring round help someone to regain consciousness
bring up raise (children)

burst in suddenly enter a room noisily
call off cancel
call on visit (a person)
call up order people to join the army
catch on become popular
●understand
catch up with draw level with (cars, runners, etc.)
check in register (at a hotel or airport)
check out hand in your keys and leave a hotel
check over see if everything is in order
clear off leave somewhere quickly

clear up tidy
●stop raining
come across find or meet by chance
come off succeed (in a plan)
come round regain consciousness
come up against be faced with
count on depend on
cut back reduce (expenditure)
cut down reduce (expenditure, consumption)
cut off stop flow of, disconnect (e.g. gas, electricity)
die away fade

do out of stop someone from having
draw up prepare a written document
●slow down and stop (in a vehicle)
drop in visit someone without warning
drop off go to sleep
fall for be very much attracted to

fall out quarrel
fall through come to nothing (plans)
get away with not to be punished
get back return
●recover possession of
get down make someone feel depressed

get off not be injured or punished when this seems likely
get out of avoid
get over recover from (e.g. sorrow, illness)
get round find a way of overcoming a difficulty
●persuade someone to let you have your way
get through pass a test or examination
give away reveal information about
give in surrender
give up surrender
●stop doing something
go down with catch an illness or disease
go in for take part in

go off become bad (e.g. food, milk)
●explode (e.g. a bomb, a firework)
go through check
hang on wait
hang up finish a telephone conversation
hold up cause delay
join in take part in
keep out of not become involved
knock out cause to become unconscious
●eliminate
let down disappoint
let off allow someone to be released from duty
●not punish someone
●cause something to explode

live up to reach the expected standard
look after take care of
look for try to find
look into investigate
look out be careful
look up try to find information (e.g. in a book)
look up to have respect for

make out manage to read or understand
make up invent or compose
make up for compensate for

pass away die
pass out lose consciousness
pay off settle a debt
pull down demolish
pull out of withdraw from (a deal or arrangement)
pull up stop (in a vehicle)
put aside save
put by save
put off postpone
put on dress
•gain (weight)
•switch on (e.g. a light, a fire)
put out switch off (e.g. a light, a fire)

put through connect (by telephone)
put up with tolerate
rub out remove (writing, a pencil drawing)
run down knock down (e.g. a pedestrian, or animal)
•lose power (e.g. a battery, a clockwork motor)
•criticize
run into bump into
•meet by chance
run out of exhaust the supply of
run over knock down (e.g. a pedestrian, an animal)
see about organize

see off go to say goodbye (e.g. at the station or airport)
see through recognize the truth (when someone is being dishonest)
send on forward (letters)

set back delay progress
set off start a journey
set out start a journey
set up establish
show off behave in a conceited way
stand out be noticeable or much better than others
stand up for defend against attack
stand up to endure hard wear
take after resemble (e.g. your mother or father)
take in fool
take off remove (e.g. a lid, clothes)
•leave the ground (e.g. a plane)

take on accept responsibility for
take up begin to spend your time doing
think up invent
throw out get rid of
turn down reduce light or volume of sound
•refuse (e.g. a job, an offer)
turn up increase light or volume of sound
•appear without warning
wear off gradually disappear
wear out become too old to use
wipe off remove with a cloth, etc.
wipe out destroy completely
work out make a plan